BED AND BREAKFAST
NEW ZEALAND

Bed and Breakfast
NEW ZEALAND

by
ELIZABETH
HANSEN

Chronicle Books ■ San Francisco

Printed in the United States of America.

Library of Congress Cataloging-in-Publication Data

Hansen, Elizabeth.
    Bed and breakfast New Zealand.

    Includes index.
    1. Bed and breakfast accommodations—New Zealand—
Guide-books. 2. New Zealand—Description and travel—
1981-   —Guide-books. I. Title.
TX910.N45H36   1987   647'.94931   87-19378
ISBN 0-87701-410-8 (pbk.)

Editing: Ellen Setteducati
Book design and art direction: Nielsen/O'Brien
Cover illustration: Hank Osuna
Text illustrations: Andrew Nielsen
Composition: Skillful Means Press

Distributed in Canada by
Raincoast Books
112 Third Avenue
Vancouver, B.C.
V5T 1C8

10 9 8 7 6 5 4 3 2 1

Chronicle Books
San Francisco, California

*For my New Zealand hosts
with sincere thanks for their
gracious hospitality*

TABLE OF CONTENTS

Introduction

The Real Down Under Wonders

New Zealand. Just the mention of the name conjures up visions of sparkling blue lakes, snow white glaciers, and majestic fiords. Geysers, bubbling mud pools, cloud-piercing mountains, and graceful willows lining grassy river banks flood the mind's eye.

Good news: it's all true. The images conveyed by travel posters, magazines, and word of mouth realistically depict New Zealand's scenic wonders. In fact, the small down under nation is even prettier than her pictures.

However, what many Americans don't realize is that New Zealand's greatest wonders aren't scenic. Her greatest assets and most memorable wonders are her people.

Kiwis, as they call themselves after their famous flightless bird, have an unsurpassed talent for making visitors feel welcome. No other country can match New Zealand's standards for hospitality and friendliness.

Happily, it isn't difficult for overseas travelers to meet local people. Overnight stays in bed and breakfast inns, country lodges, historic hotels, and private homes and farms are easily arranged. Each of these alternative forms of accommodations provides an opportunity for guests to savor the famed Kiwi hospitality.

Since the people are what make New Zealand special, staying in a high-rise hotel or one of the ubiquitous chain motels would be akin to fasting in France, teetotaling at Oktoberfest, or avoiding *el sol* on the Mexican Riviera.

As in other parts of the world, the contrasts between traditional and alternative styles of lodging in New Zealand are readily apparent. In a hotel a knock on your door early in the morning will be an employee wanting to check the mini-bar. At a farm stay it will be your hostess bringing in early-morning tea. Which would you prefer?

In addition to superb hospitality, alternative accommodations have other advantages. The most evident of these are delicious meals. The breakfasts served at B & Bs sustain a traveler through most of the day. The gourmet game foods presented at country lodges are rarely found on the menus of hotel dining rooms. Microwaved motor-inn fare pales in comparison with fresh farm produce.

Visitors who stay where they have a host or hostess also have an advantage when it comes to sightseeing and shopping. Only the locals know about the fascinating little museums that aren't mentioned in guidebooks and the bargains available in area shops.

A Matter of Semantics

Lots of things are different in New Zealand. Winter starts in June, and Christmas comes in the middle of summer. The warmest weather is in the northern part of the country. Water goes down the drain counterclockwise. Considering these facts, it isn't surprising that the Kiwi version of bed and breakfast and the semantics used by New Zealanders to describe various types of lodging differ from those of other nations.

The biggest confusion arises when the term *private hotel* is used. For a long time I thought that these must be members-only places, and consequently I avoided them. What I came to realize, however, is that a private hotel in New Zealand is one that isn't licensed to serve alcohol. From the American point of view, a New Zealand private hotel is a *bed and breakfast inn*. Private hotels are also known as *guest houses* and *travel hotels*, but the term *bed and breakfast inn* is gradually becoming accepted.

The typical B & B described in this book has five or more bedrooms, either with attached baths or, more commonly, with showers and toilets down the hall. The rooms don't have telephones or televisions, but they're always clean and neat. A bed and breakfast is a great place for meeting other travelers — either at breakfast or over a cup of tea in the parlor.

Tariffs range from $14 for a single without a private bath (but including breakfast and taxes) to $60 for a room for two with attached bath. Dinner may be available for an extra charge.

Whereas the inns are similar to those found in the United States and Britain, another popular type of lodging, the *farm stay*, isn't found in many other countries. In this case, visitors become the house guests of a rural family and can either participate in the daily farm routine or go off exploring the surrounding area on their own.

The homes vary in size and amenities but generally exceed the guests' expectations. Unlike the U.S., where a wealthy farmer is the exception rather than the rule, in New Zealand farmers historically have controlled much of the country's wealth. Many farm homesteads are furnished with valuable antiques and offer such features as swimming pools and tennis courts.

The farmer and his wife are usually well educated and knowledgeable about such things as world affairs, classical music, and international travel.

Why do they invite visitors on a paying-guest

basis? Partly because their children have gone off to boarding school and left them with an empty nest, but moreover because they genuinely enjoy meeting overseas travelers.

Unlike farm stays in Britain, where only bed and breakfast are provided, New Zealand farm stays provide accommodations and all meals. The rates vary from $25 to $75 per person and, in most cases, also include morning and afternoon tea, wine with dinner, and a tour of the property. Generally speaking, the higher price is charged when gourmet fare and fine wines are served and when the house is particularly grand and well appointed.

A *home stay* is similar to a farm stay, except that it's located in or near an urban area. The tariff for a home stay may include only bed and breakfast if there are restaurants nearby.

Bed and breakfast inns, home stays, and farm stays are all economical types of accommodations in New Zealand; *country lodges* cater to more affluent travelers. Originally designed to meet the needs of fishermen and hunters, the lodges now pamper an international clientele whose only common bond is an interest in the best of everything money can buy. Sporting activities still abound, but equal priority is now given to cordon bleu cuisine and the best New Zealand and imported wines. Helicopter pads, experienced fishing guides, and chauffeur-driven limousines are provided as required.

Because of their secluded locations, the lodges operate on "an all-inclusive" basis. The tariffs, which vary from $200 to $360 for two, include meals, cocktails, wine, and a great deal of personal attention.

I've also selected some interesting *historic hotels* for inclusion in this book. They differ from the farm stays, home stays, bed and breakfast inns, and country lodges in that the host's involvement with guests is minimal. However, because their bars are open to the public, the historic hotels provide a good opportunity for visitors to mix with locals on a very casual basis and experience authentic country-pub ambiance.

Kiwis *are* the country's greatest wonder, and nowhere are they more wonderful than in the pub.

A Crash Course in Kiwi

I did a double take the first time the proprietor of a B & B inquired, "Shall I knock you up in the morning, dearie?" It took me a second to realize he was offering to wake me.

I drew a blank stare from my hostess on a farm stay when I asked for my eggs "sunny-side up." She was only too happy to comply with my request after I explained what I meant.

Rarely do the differences in American English and Kiwi English render the parties involved unable to communicate. More often they provide a few laughs and a good conversation starter.

Throughout this book, you'll notice I've put the Kiwi equivalent to our American terms in parentheses. The following are a few other new meanings you might watch out for:

bathroom — where one bathes (if you want the toilet, ask for it by name)

biscuits — cookies

cooked breakfast — usually bacon and eggs (pancakes, French toast, etc., are rare)

Continental breakfast — cereal, toast, juice, fruit, coffee, tea

drawing room — formal living room

duvet ("due-vay") — comforter, quilt

electric blankets — in New Zealand they're found under the bottom sheet

en suite facilities — attached bath

entree — small first course

homely — homey

hotties — hot water bottles

jelly — gelatine dessert (Jell-O)

jersey — sweater

lemonade — 7-Up

loo — toilet

lounge — living room or parlor

main course — entree

Milo — a hot drink similar to Ovaltine

muesli — granola

napkin — diaper

pub — public-licensed hotel, a place to drink

private facilities (pf) — private bath

rates — property taxes

serviette — napkin

single bed — twin bed

spa bath — a bathtub with whirlpool jets

spa pool — Jacuzzi, hot tub

station — large farm, ranch

surname — last name

tariffs — rates

tea — the national beverage; also, colloquially, "dinner"

toast rack — used to cool toast (so butter won't melt!)

white tea — tea with milk

A Word About Rates

Rather than quote rates in exact dollar amounts, I've established five price categories. It is important to note what meals and other expenses are included. For instance, an inn (bed and breakfast) that costs $30 for two and is therefore labeled inexpensive is actually the same value as a farm stay that costs $50 for two and is categorized as moderate. The difference is, of course, that the rate at the farm stay includes all meals and wine with dinner.

Prices in U.S. dollars, including applicable taxes and based on two people sharing a room, are as follows: inexpensive — less than $35; moderate — $35 – 80; moderately expensive — $80 – 160; expensive — $160 – 265; very expensive — more than $265.

The single rate for farm stays and most home stays is half the double rate. In the case of country lodges, bed and breakfast inns, and historic hotels, the single rate is one-half to two-thirds the tariff for two.

A Few Suggestions

Try to book home stays and farm stays at least forty-eight hours in advance of your arrival.

Confirm rates at time of booking.

Let your host know in advance if there's something you're particularly interested in doing.

Arrange your trip so you can stay two consecutive nights at the same farm stay.

Pack a wash cloth, some tissues, a bathrobe, a travel alarm clock, dual-voltage appliances, and an adaptor plug for Kiwi electrical outlets.

Drink the water.

Take more than one credit card. The major ones accepted in New Zealand are American Express, MasterCard (Bankcard), Visa, and Diners Club. Take any two of these and you'll be fine.

Take some small gifts (pictorial calendars, tea towels, illustrated booklets with pictures of your hometown, etc.) to show your appreciation for special kindness.

While your trip is in the planning stages, write to New Zealand Tourist and Publicity (10960 Wilshire Blvd., Suite 1530, Los Angeles, CA 90024) for information and maps.

Be courteous. Be on time for meals, tidy up after

yourself in the bathroom, and be ready to depart by midmorning.

If traveling in winter, keep in mind that central heating is rare in New Zealand.

Don't ever treat your host like a household servant.

Don't pack a travel iron; they're readily available.

Don't tip.

Don't expect to find king-size beds.

Reservations

The most popular period for travel to New Zealand is from November to March. During this time, and especially for the busy month of January, it is advisable to make advance reservations ("pre-book") for at least some of your accommodations.

The most inexpensive way to do this is to write directly to the property at which you'd like to stay. Allow ten days for your letter to arrive, and keep in mind that air mail to New Zealand from the U.S. costs forty-four cents per *half* ounce.

It's much faster, but more costly (about $5 for three minutes), to phone (ring) the property. To do this, dial 011 (international access), 64 (the country code for New Zealand), and the number desired.

The part of the telephone number in parentheses is the STD code, which is the equivalent of our area code. When dialing from the U.S., omit the first number of the STD code if it is 0.

For example, if you were phoning Ellerton Lodge (near Auckland) from the United States, you would dial 011-64-(9)-450-484.

If you were in New Zealand, but not in Auckland, you would dial (09)-450-484.

And if you were in Auckland, you would omit the STD code altogether and just dial 450-484.

Your travel agent can also make reservations for you by phoning New Zealand Central Reservations. Their toll-free numbers are (800) 351-2317 (in California) or (800) 351-2323 (nationwide). Although they take reservations only via agents, they do dispense general travel information to consumers.

When you make your reservations, check the rate and ask about acceptable forms of payment.

If you are traveling at a busy time of the year, it's possible that the home stays and farm stays of your choice will be unavailable. In that case, I suggest you contact one of the companies listed in the Appendix and let them make alternate arrangements for you.

A Personal Note

My personal love affair with New Zealand began in 1975 during a brief stopover on my way to Australia. The moment I stepped off the plane I knew I'd arrived in a very special place. I don't know if it was the smell of the freshly washed air, the sight of the smiling customs agents, the sound of the Kiwi accent, or a combination of all three, but I had the sense of having come home.

Since then, I've returned nine times. I've escorted groups of American tourists through the country, researched and written dozens of articles for various magazines and newspapers, and, in 1984, wrote my first book, *The Woman's Travel Guide to New Zealand*.

My fondness for New Zealand has never dwindled, but there were times while I was doing the research for this book when I felt like I was falling in love all over again. I think it was because I spent much of my time in rural areas with down-to-earth people and saw more clearly than ever that this is where the real beauty of the country lies.

It isn't surprising that as the tourist industry grows

in New Zealand, there is an increasing proliferation of commercial attractions and high-rise hotels. My hope is that by using *Bed and Breakfast: New Zealand* you'll be able to find your way off the beaten path and into the homes, the inns, the lodges, and the hearts of New Zealanders.

SOUTH ISLAND

NORTH ISLAND

Bay of Islands

Paihia • Russell

Dargaville •

GREAT
BARRIER
ISLAND

Warkworth
Auckland • Whitianga

• Thames   Bay of Plenty

Mount Maunganni

Teawamutu • • Cambridge

Rotorua   Ruatoria

Taupo   Tolaga Bay

Turangi •   Gisborne

• Kaponga   Hawke Bay
Napier

Hastings •
Wanganui •

• Kimbolton
• Marton   • Dannevirke
• Palmerston North

• Masterton

Wellington
Palliser Bay

Auckland and Vicinity

It doesn't take visitors long to understand why Auckland is known as the "city of sails." The sparkling waters of Waitemata Harbor are dotted with boats nearly every day of the week, providing New Zealand's largest city (pop. 800,000) with a beautiful backdrop.

Another appropriate and comprehensible motto might be "city of contrasts," because Auckland is at once British and Polynesian, rural and urban, sophisticated and ingenuous.

White-wigged jurists in traditional black robes and Samoans in colorful clothes are equally common sights on the city's streets. High-rise buildings fill the downtown area, but sheep graze nearby. Gourmet restaurants and quality theater are well attended, as is the annual Easter Show of handicrafts and agricultural products.

It is a city with a sense of humor (a naked runner was the highlight of a recent ten-kilometer race) and a serious side (which seems appropriate for the nation's major industrial center and trade gateway).

These contradictions work together to make Auckland a lively, colorful city. Visitors who stop over on their way to adventures in other parts of the country discover that the contrasts help to make the "city of sails" a city of many options and pleasant surprises.

Some people are happy walking along the harbor, where cargo ships from all over the world are unloaded; others enjoy a few hours on one of the tourist boats; the most adventuresome choose to leave the city behind and explore the nearby islands: Waiheke, Rangitoto, Pakatoa, and Great Barrier.

In addition to the islands, the Coromandel Peninsula provides another refreshing destination for visitors who want to experience rural New Zealand within a short distance of Auckland.

ASCOT PARNELL

36 St. Stephens Avenue
Parnell, Auckland 1, (09) 399-012
■

HOSTS: Heidi and Alfred Hassencamp.
LOCATION: Central Auckland.
CATEGORY: Bed and breakfast inn.
ACCOMMODATIONS: Nine rooms, all with private bath.
RATES: Inexpensive.
INCLUDED: Breakfast.
CREDIT CARDS: All major.

Heidi and Alfred Hassencamp aren't about to let grass grow under their feet. They immigrated from Germany in 1984, and by Christmas of that year they had bought a large, elegant private home in Auckland's Parnell district and turned it into a B & B. When I first saw the Ascot Parnell, the rooms lacked telephones and bathrooms, but the new owners lost no time in having them added.

Fortunately, the renovations have been completed without altering the home's original elegant features. The marble lighting fixture hanging in one bathroom is at least eighty years old, as is the beautiful crystal chandelier in the dining room.

Room one has an impressive ceiling made of rimu, a native timber, but my favorite is room six, in which the slanted ceiling and leaded windows create a cozy atmosphere.

The gardens surrounding the Ascot Parnell are a horticulturist's delight. Palm, fig, and passion-fruit trees grow alongside citrus, banana, and rimu. There's even a registered historic tree — a large pin oak reputed to be over 130 years old.

When the Hassencamps noticed that their guests enjoyed climbing the tree, they placed a ladder nearby to help them.

"They just love it," Heidi told me. "Sometimes they hang in it like cherries."

The accommodating attitude of the hosts is one of the reasons this bed and breakfast inn is very popular. Another contributing factor is its location in Parnell, an area where handicrafts shops, boutiques, restaurants, and tearooms abound. It's an easy walk to the Rose Garden on Gladstone Road, the War Memorial Museum, or the Parnell Pools. The city center is a comfortable mile and a half away.

Guests who meet over a cup of tea in the parlor often get together for dinner at a nearby restaurant. Fiddlers, which is located, not surprisingly, on a roof, is a frequent choice because they serve traditional New Zealand fare (roasts, lamb cutlets, local fish, etc.).

I'm a great fan of Devonshire tea (scones with cream and raspberry jam), so when I'm in Parnell I head for the Turret Cafe, located upstairs in Parnell Village.

Because there are many dining spots in the neighborhood, Heidi and Alfred normally don't offer meals other than breakfast. However, on a "nasty, rainy day" Heidi makes a "big, hot pot" for dinner, and those who don't want to brave the weather are welcome to dine at home.

As if they weren't busy enough just cooking for and graciously accommodating their guests, the Hassencamps even go to the downtown airport terminal to collect new arrivals.

It's easy to understand why the Ascot Parnell is frequently full (chock-a-block) in the height of the season. Potential guests should follow the Hassencamps' example and not let grass grow under their feet while thinking about making advance reservations.

ASPEN LODGE

62 Emily Place
Auckland, (09) 796-698
■

HOST: Paul Petersen.

LOCATION: Central Auckland.

CATEGORY: Bed and breakfast inn.

ACCOMMODATIONS: Twenty-three rooms, none with private bath.

RATES: Inexpensive.

INCLUDED: Breakfast.

CREDIT CARDS: All major.

RESTRICTIONS: No children.

Paul Petersen has good reason to refer to the dining room at his Aspen Lodge as "the little UN." On any given morning there will be Germans, Japanese, Dutch, and Australians (Aussies), as well as Americans and Canadians, enjoying their Continental breakfast and exchanging information. Because of its low rates and central location, this B & B appeals to budget travelers of all ages who are using public transportation to get around New Zealand.

Those who arrive by air take the Airporter shuttle bus ($3.50) to the Hyatt Kingsgate Hotel and then walk the short distance to Aspen Lodge. Queen Street, Auckland's main thoroughfare, is also less than a five-minute walk, as are the bus terminal and train station.

The New Zealand Tourist and Publicity office, at 99 Queen Street, and the Auckland Visitors Bureau, located farther up the same street, are both good sources of information on local sightseeing. Bus excursions that highlight the city's main attractions (Kelly Tarlton's Underwater World, the War Memorial Museum, Victoria Park Market, the Museum of Transport and Technology, and Heritage Park) can be arranged at either place.

Visitors who only have time to do one thing in Auckland should go to the War Memorial Museum to see its collection of Maori artifacts and carvings. Admission is free, and it has a very good souvenir and craft shop.

Tourists who want to get out on the water can take the ferry to Devonport, sail on the Pride of Auckland (a sixty-foot catamaran that does two-hour sightseeing cruises), or enjoy the Captain Cook Lunch Cruise.

Queen Street is one of the best areas for shopping and offers a wide variety of restaurants, theaters, and nightclubs.

Since Paul's background includes experience in the local hotel and restaurant business, he's a wealth of information when it comes to choosing a place to dine. No matter what the request, he seems to enjoy helping. As he put it, "I'm a people person."

During my last visit to the Aspen Lodge, a guest was gloating over a rare camera he'd just purchased, and he gave his host the credit for telling him about the shop in which he'd found it.

Paul and his partner Chris Alpe purchased the three-story Aspen Lodge in April 1986 and are gradually refurbishing it. They plan to redo the bedrooms with pine furniture and fresh curtains; new beds are already in place.

At the present time the breakfast room, where coffee- and tea-making facilities are provided, is also used for watching television, and another parlor is set aside for reading, writing post cards, and such. An inviting sitting area on the back lawn is popular in the summer, and a garden conservatory will soon be added.

"The bedrooms are modest," Paul admitted, "but our international clientele doesn't seem to mind. They seem to feel that our location and friendly atmosphere are more important than up-market amenities."

CHALET CHEVRON TOURIST HOTEL

14 Brighton Road
Parnell, Auckland, (09) 390-290

■

HOSTS: Laurel and Norm Peden.

LOCATION: Central Auckland.

CATEGORY: Bed and breakfast inn.

ACCOMMODATIONS: Thirteen rooms, all with private bath.

RATES: Inexpensive.

INCLUDED: Breakfast.

CREDIT CARDS: All major.

I think it's the little reception desk in the foyer and the wide, carpeted staircase leading up to the bedrooms that give the Chalet Chevron the ambiance of a small European hotel. And the feeling is reinforced by the glass doors that lead from the entrance hall to the parlor.

The aura is so strong that when I first looked out at the harbor through the floor-to-ceiling windows in the dining room, I had to remind myself I wasn't looking at the Bay of Sorrento or the Amalfi coast.

However, the arrival of a very un-Continental breakfast brought me to my senses. Norm Peden likes to serve hearty Kiwi fare to his guests. This means they have a choice of bacon and eggs, poached eggs, baked beans on toast, or spaghetti on toast, in addition to juice, cereal, fruit, and coffee or tea. The meal is complemented by the sunny room, with red plush chairs and carpeting, in which it's served and by the expansive harbor view.

The Pedens also offer three-course dinners — usually soup followed by a roast and dessert — at an extra charge of about $7.

Upstairs, most of the bedrooms have the same lovely harbor outlook as the dining room. Number seven has an especially good view, and rooms one and three have views from both bed and bathrooms. Norm likes to say they have "a loo with a view."

All of the accommodations, which are on three levels, are bright and cheerful, and each room has its own telephone and radio. (The rooms on the lower level are the smaller singles.) Three bathrooms have tubs; the others have showers. The furnishings are circa 1950, probably because that was the year the house, which was built in 1924, was converted from a private home to an inn. The exterior is freshly painted white frame with double gables, reminiscent of a storybook cottage.

One Kiwi businessman has been staying at the Chalet Chevron once a month for thirty years, but most guests are overseas travelers who have just arrived in the country.

"Sometimes I've been in the lounge [parlor] and heard a half dozen languages going at one time," Norm told me. "It's a real league of nations."

Luckily for his guests, Norm Peden is a likable, friendly person who takes his role of self-appointed ambassador seriously. As he explained it, "I might be the first New Zealander a visitor meets, and I want them to get off to a good start." Even Heide, the resident Weimaraner, does her best to make guests feel welcome.

The inn is located about a mile and a half from the center of Auckland. The Pedens don't provide courtesy-car transfers, but they're only a short taxi ride from the various downtown transportation terminals.

Apparently, I'm not the only one who feels the European ambiance at the Chalet Chevron. Norm told me that given their choice of all the restaurants in the area, his guests seem to gravitate to the Chianti and pasta served at La Trattoria on Parnell Road.

AACHEN HOUSE

39 Market Road
Remuera, Auckland; (09) 502-329
■

HOSTS: Sandie and Richard Rice.
LOCATION: Suburban Auckland.
CATEGORY: Bed and breakfast inn.
ACCOMMODATIONS: Seven rooms, none with private bath.
RATES: Inexpensive.
INCLUDED: Breakfast.
CREDIT CARDS: MasterCard and Visa.

At first it seems incongruous that a couple who chose to live in New Zealand because they like "the slower, easier way of life" and because "it's a good place to bring up children" would also choose to open a bed and breakfast inn. After all, many B & Bs don't even accept children, and, although the hosts may appear relaxed in front of the guests, running an inn is hardly an easy way of life.

But Sandie and Richard Rice have not only been able to combine raising a family and operating Aachen House, they've also managed to blend the two into a mutually beneficial situation.

There are no Do Not Touch signs in this comfortable two-story Victorian. Instead, children and adults are welcome to treat the house as a home away from home. There's a cozy open fire in the living room during the winter, and lots of card and board games are available for rainy afternoons. In better weather young guests join the Rices' four offspring on a trampoline in the back yard.

Sandie and Richard introduce folks who haven't yet met, and everyone sits together for breakfast. Because the family atmosphere promotes conversation, the hosts have become thoroughly conversant in American English. Guests are offered eggs "sunny-side up," "over easy," and so on. Also in response to American visitors, perked coffee and ice water are available.

Desserts are the favorite feature of the home-cooked dinners, which are available for an additional charge of about $7. Sandie makes a wonderful steamed fruit pudding and a special cheesecake that, according to Richard, is "at least four inches high."

Normally, lunch isn't offered at Aachen House, but the hosts will prepare a picnic (cut lunch) if it's requested. This is just one of the generous "extras" Sandie and Richard do for their guests. They also pick up and deliver people from and to the airport, help to arrange sightseeing and shopping excursions, and provide advice on rental cars, accommodations in other parts of New Zealand, and public transportation. And, to my knowledge, theirs is the only Kiwi B & B that makes high chairs and baby beds (cots) available.

The Rices chose to live in New Zealand after trying out several other places. Sandie, whose mother is English and whose father is a New Zealander, was born in Bombay and educated in West Pakistan. Her parents now live in Japan. She met Richard, a Kiwi, while they were both living in England. Needless to say, they love traveling and enjoy sharing experiences with their house guests, who sometimes feel more as if they're staying in a private home than an inn.

Because of the family atmosphere, it seems appropriate that bedroom doors lock only from the inside, that seven rooms share three bathrooms, and that the furnishings are serviceable but not fancy.

The two front rooms overlook Hobson Park, and three sunny back rooms have a view of the lawn and flower garden. Each has a sink (hand basin) and an electrical outlet for shavers.

Land hockey is played in Hobson Park during the winter, and Alexander Park, which has night harness racing (the trots) year-round, is a fifteen-minute walk away. Many visitors take the short hike to the top of nearby Mount Hobson for a good view of the city, which is about five miles away. It's also fun to walk around the neighborhood and look at grand Victorian homes and their pretty gardens.

There's regular bus service into the city, and Remuera, which is considered a rather posh suburb, also has some interesting shops and good restaurants.

The Hong Kong Seafood Restaurant on Great South Road is a popular BYO (bring your own wine or beer). However, even though I adore Cantonese fish dishes, it's hard to give up an evening with the Rices and their "slower, easier way of life."

Aachen House

ELLERTON LODGE

39 Clarence Street
Devonport, Auckland, (09) 450-484
■

HOSTS: Beverly and John Hoskins.
LOCATION: Suburban Auckland.
CATEGORY: Country lodge.
ACCOMMODATIONS: One one-bedroom suite and two
two-bedroom suites, each with private bath.
RATES: Expensive.
INCLUDED: Breakfast, pre-dinner cocktails, coffee and brandy
after dinner.
CREDIT CARDS: All major.

I've categorized Ellerton as a "country lodge" in spite of the fact
that it isn't in the country. It is, in fact, located in Devonport, only
a twelve-minute ferry ride across the harbor from Auckland.
However, Ellerton is one of those rare suburban places that has
the qualities usually offered only by country lodges: beautiful
natural surroundings, gracious hospitality, and personal attention.
The state of mind, the sense of being pampered, that prevails
among guests at a good country lodge is also prevalent at Ellerton.

John and Beverly Hoskins are responsible for the success of
Ellerton Lodge. They have remodeled the garden level of their
rambling white mansion into three elegantly furnished, self-
contained suites and devote themselves fully to "mollycoddling"
visitors from all over the world.

The personal attention starts with tea and homemade scones,
served to guests in a sunny sitting area overlooking the harbor.
This vantage point provides an expansive view of downtown
Auckland, ships going in and out of port, and the Devonport
waterfront.

John and Beverly set about making arrangements for the new
arrivals as soon as they determine their guests' interests. These
may include golf, sailing, fishing, touring vineyards, sightseeing
(by car or helicopter), or just relaxing around the lodge.

When time permits, they also invite local people who share
hobbies or occupations with their guests to come for pre-dinner
drinks. Stock brokers meet stock brokers, tennis players meet

tennis players, and so forth. This is a unique opportunity for overseas visitors to sample the lifestyle of New Zealand's gentry. These cocktail parties are held in John's "pub," a handsome barroom overlooking the swimming pool.

In the dining room next to the bar, the hosts serve their guests sumptuous breakfasts at a table set with bone china, silver, and damask napkins. The emphasis is on fresh fruit, but English sausages, country bacon, and eggs any style are always available. Given enough time, John and Beverly will also try to fill special requests. One diplomat mentioned that he particularly enjoyed croissants in the morning, and John phoned all over town to find out who made the best ones.

Dinner is available if required, but with more than half a dozen good restaurants close to Ellerton, hardly anyone ever asks to dine in. Instead, John drives guests to and from the restaurant, and when they return to their suite, coffee, brandy, and homemade chocolates are waiting.

Devonport offers more than just a wide selection of restaurants. The quiet Edwardian suburb is home to many artists and craftspeople, and shops that sell their wares are tucked around the village. A path along the sea front invites walkers and joggers, and two local museums are open daily.

Ellerton Lodge, which was one of the first houses in Devonport, was built in 1871 and has been in Beverly's family since the turn of the century. It is tastefully furnished with crystal chandeliers, brocade bedspreads, silk draperies, and imported wallpapers. In one suite, French doors opening onto a brick patio provide a commanding view of lush lawn, flower gardens, the harbor, and the city.

Guests strolling around the grounds discover a swimming pool, a hot tub (spa pool), a cold plunge pool, and a solarium covered with colorful bougainvillea. Each suite has a small kitchen, a color television, and a private telephone.

Prior to departing, guests are invited to add a bottle of wine to Ellerton's cellar. The bottle is labeled and remains in the cellar until it can be enjoyed on a later visit or claimed by a friend who is also lucky enough to be a guest at this lovely "country" lodge.

GROWSE HOUSE

13 Allender Drive
Torbay, Auckland; (09) 404-6603

∎

HOSTS: Bonnie and Jeremy Rees-Webbe.

LOCATION: Suburban Auckland.

CATEGORY: Home stay.

ACCOMMODATIONS: One room with private bath.

RATES: Moderate.

INCLUDED: All meals, wine with dinner.

CREDIT CARDS: None.

Bonnie and Jeremy Rees-Webbe refer to their home stay as "an experience in living with New Zealanders." Guests are treated like personal friends and are encouraged to "join in our lives, be part of the family." The Rees-Webbes even welcome visitors to share holidays with them, their two teen-age children, and other relatives who live in the area. This is a great opportunity for people who enjoy becoming more than superficially involved with their host.

Jeremy is an airline pilot, but when they have visitors staying he takes time off from work to be with them. Since he has to schedule these days well ahead of time, they prefer to receive reservation requests a month in advance of arrival.

Because Jeremy flies for an internal airline, he is well acquainted with both the North Island and the South Island, and he likes helping house guests plan their itinerary through the country. He even has a twenty-minute video about New Zealand that he can show.

The Rees-Webbes enjoy taking their guests to the hot pools at Waiwera, a half-hour's drive away, and hiking (tramping) in the Waitakere Ranges. They also take people into Auckland for sightseeing, and, closer to home, they help their overseas arrivals recover from jet lag with a walk on Long Bay Beach.

Torbay, a modern upper-middle-class suburb, is a twenty-minute drive from the city center. Because of the hosts' willingness to show people around, visitors don't need to have their own car.

The Rees-Webbe's home was "named" by an unknowing construction worker who, while working on the site, was overheard to say, "Jeez, this is really a growse house." (In Aussie-Kiwi slang, *growse* is used to describe anything that's really good.)

While I wouldn't have chosen the same word, I agree that the two-story house with its tasteful traditional furnishings is very attractive. The guest room has a double bed and a twin; the bathroom reserved for guests is across the hall.

The house is surrounded by four and a half acres of land, which enables Bonnie and Jeremy to produce their own vegetables, fruit, honey, and eggs. As a result, Bonnie's blackberry pie, peach pie, and homemade jam are really delicious.

The hostess also prepares a special granola (muesli), which guests enjoy at breakfast, and she likes to serve homemade pizza for lunch. Traditional New Zealand dishes, like roast lamb, are featured at dinner time. Easter company is treated to freshly baked hot cross buns.

The Rees-Webbes have a mixed national background and welcome people from any nation to their home. Bonnie is a Kiwi, but Jeremy has English parents and was born in Zanzibar. He traveled throughout the world with the merchant navy before settling in New Zealand. One of his ancestors was the first governor of Virginia in 1617.

It's not surprising that guests who have spent a few days at Growse House feel like a member of the family and are often misty-eyed when they leave. My time with the Rees-Webbes was short, but even so, I noticed a distinct lump in my throat as I backed my car out of their driveway.

TEN TAUMATA ROAD

10 Taumata Road
Castor Bay, Auckland 9; (09) 469-363

■

HOSTS: Helen Pasalich and Neville McLindon.

LOCATION: Suburban Auckland.

CATEGORY: Home stay.

ACCOMMODATIONS: Two rooms share one bath.

RATES: Inexpensive.

INCLUDED: Breakfast.

CREDIT CARDS: None.

The Pasalich-McLindon home stay is a dream come true for active people who'd like to sample the Kiwi sporting life with local hosts. Helen plays tennis and Mac plays golf, and they both enjoy hiking and sailing (yachting). Helen summed it up when she said, "We're really outdoor people."

When I asked Mac, a retired air traffic controller, if he plays golf with visitors, his Irish eyes lit up and he began describing some of the courses to which he likes to take guests. Apparently, his favorite is the seaside course at Muriwai. (New Zealand has more than three hundred golf courses; green fees are about $3 per game.) Helen was just as enthusiastic about taking guests to the tennis club in Castor Bay, and they both rhapsodized about hiking in local woodland areas and along nearby beaches. Although they don't own their own sailboat, one is available to them during the summer.

Mac and Helen will also take guests sightseeing and shopping if they don't have their own car. The tour of Auckland starts with a drive up One Tree Hill, one of the many volcanic cones on which the city is built. When it's time for shopping, Helen knows where to find bargains on sweaters and other New Zealand handicrafts.

Sheepskins are a favorite purchase for overseas visitors, and Breen's on Quay (pronounced "Key") Street has a very good selection and competitive prices. They sell skins only from the Bowron Tannery, "because they're the best." Bowron skins are star-graded, which means there's a star on the back with a number in it. The numbers (2–6) indicate the size of the skin and the depth of the pile. All star-graded skins are the same quality.

The second-best skins, after Bowron, are Windward. They also come in various sizes and are a little less expensive.

House guests who prefer to be on their own can take the bus into town. The seven-mile trip from Castor Bay takes about twenty minutes.

The two guest rooms in the contemporary home that Mac and Helen share were created when children, now grown, moved out on their own. The upstairs room has twin beds, and the downstairs room has one single bed. There's a cozy fire in the living room on winter days and a peak view of the islands in the Hauraki Gulf when the weather is clear.

An evening meal with wine is provided for an extra charge of about $7. During the summer, this might be fish and salad or barbecued steak or lamb chops. The hosts also enjoy going to local restaurants with their house guests. In either case, visitors are bound to have a good time; Helen is lively and gregarious, and Mac's a real charmer who's full of interesting tales about life on Cyprus and other places he's lived.

They're both agreeable to accepting reservations on short notice, but, knowing these two, I wouldn't recommend waiting until the last minute to contact them. Neither one of them is the type who'd sit around waiting for the phone to ring.

FITZROY HOUSE

Port Fitzroy
Great Barrier Island; Port Fitzroy 2
■

HOSTS: Heather and David Palmer.
LOCATION: Hauraki Gulf, fifty-six miles northeast of Auckland.
CATEGORY: Bed and breakfast inn.
ACCOMMODATIONS: Nine rooms, two with private bath.
RATES: Moderate.
INCLUDED: All meals.
CREDIT CARDS: MasterCard, Visa.

"The Barrier," as the locals call it, lies fifty-six miles across the water from Auckland. It has less than five hundred inhabitants, a frustrating, antiquated telephone system, and roads that would be an embarrassment in a Third World country. On the other hand, I have never met friendlier people, eaten better seafood, or seen so many endangered species of native birds.

Depending on the individual traveler's definition of "off-the-beaten-path" (for some people it means not having twenty-four hour room service), a couple of days on Great Barrier Island might prove to be the highlight of a New Zealand vacation.

For those who decide to stay at the Port Fitzroy end of the island, I heartily recommend Fitzroy House, which overlooks the harbor. It was built in 1903 and for many years was the only building in the area. Proprietors David and Heather Palmer are both natives—David is a fourth-generation Barrier Island Maori—and you couldn't ask for nicer hosts.

Fitzroy House is set on a two-hundred-acre working farm, and guests are welcome to gather eggs or try their hand at milking a cow. The Palmers also supply fishing poles, and it's possible to catch snapper from their private jetty. Other Barrier activities include hiking, deep-sea fishing, scuba diving, boating, and bird watching. The New Zealand Forest Service conducts a program of guided walks during the summer, and charter boats can be arranged at any time of the year.

Heather and David's hearty meals provide their guests with the energy needed for island activities. At breakfast there is a choice between traditional bacon and eggs or "bubble and squeak"—patties consisting of hash browns, vegetables, and eggs.

Fresh local fish, such as snapper, tarakihi, or kahawai, and shellfish, such as mussels and lobster (crayfish), dominate the dinner menu. In addition, the hosts will prepare abalone (paua) and scallops if someone collects them. Wine is available at dinner, or guests may BYO.

When David isn't serving dinner or working on the farm, he's running minibus tours of the island. These cost about $15 and last a full day. He varies the itinerary as much as possible to suit his passengers' interests.

His tours are informative; given the condition of the roads, however, some people prefer to remain behind soaking up the old-world atmosphere of Fitzroy House and watching for native birds. Without much effort it's possible to see banded rails, fantails, fern birds, gray warblers, native pigeons, tuis, and kakas (native parrots). Elsewhere on the island I saw several endangered brown teal ducks taking a dip in a swimming pool.

In spring the golden blossoms of the kowhai tree are popular with the birds; in summertime the scarlet flowers of the pohutu-kawa, also known as the New Zealand Christmas tree, draw their attention.

Fitzroy House is open all year. The easiest way to get there is to take Sea Bee Air to Port Fitzroy. Their amphibious planes land in the harbor within sight of the inn, and David and Heather collect new arrivals from the waterfront.

These flights are a good introduction to life on Barrier Island: tattered boxes of goods belonging to passengers are stacked next to crates of supplies for the general store; a basket housing a cat who has been to the vet in Auckland might be perched on top of the Royal Mail pouch or the day's delivery of current newspapers.

On my trip to Port Fitzroy, the other passengers decided I should sit next to the pilot, and all during the flight they shouted forward bits and pieces of information about the islands over which we were flying.

Returning to Auckland, I wasn't nearly so lucky. The flight was bumpy, and my seat partner was a Great Dane with extremely bad breath.

TIPI AND BOB'S HOLIDAY HOME

R.D. 1, Tryphena
Great Barrier Island, Tryphena 5A
■

HOSTS: Tipi and Bob Whitmore.
LOCATION: Hauraki Gulf, fifty-six miles northeast of Auckland.
CATEGORY: Bed and breakfast inn.
ACCOMMODATIONS: Two rooms share one bath; separate cottage, which sleeps four, has a private bath.
RATES: Moderate.
INCLUDED: All meals, wine with dinner.
CREDIT CARDS: None.

Tipi Whitmore's cooking is so good that news of it has reached Auckland. Before I left for the Barrier, several people said to me,

"Where are you going to stay? I hear the food at Tipi and Bob's is really great."

And they were right.

For breakfast, Tipi serves bacon and eggs, tomatoes, a mixed grill, or poached fish with cheese sauce. Lunch might be a chowder made from local fish, fresh mushroom soup, or cold tongue soup accompanied by fresh bread. Between breakfast and lunch, home-baked goodies are offered with morning tea. By afternoon tea time most guests feel like overfed cruise-ship passengers, but it's all too good to pass up.

Deep-fried fish, either snapper or gurnard, is the specialty of the house, but lobster and scallops are also served when they're in season. The dinner menu could also feature roast lamb with baked sweet potato (kumara) and cauliflower with cheese sauce. Everything that comes out of Tipi's kitchen tastes terrific. (The hosts supply one complimentary glass of wine with dinner, and guests are welcome to BYO.)

The lack of restaurants and the isolation make it necessary for the inns on the island to serve all meals, not just breakfast. This gives them a cozy family feeling that would be hard to find in a city. Since there are only three guest rooms at Tipi and Bob's, the homey atmosphere is especially strong.

Like everyone else on the Barrier, the Whitmores provide their own electricity. The lights go out and electric blankets cool down when the generator is switched off at night, but the hostess thoughtfully offers hot water bottles (hotties) to her guests in the winter months.

The bedrooms in the modern house open onto a sun deck and are nicely furnished. From the spacious, comfortable living room decorated with family pictures, seascape paintings, lace tablecloths, and house plants, there is a good view of Tryphena Harbor about thirty feet away. Sometimes it's possible to see dolphins at play.

I was surprised to learn that this large house was brought on a barge from Auckland more than fifteen years ago. Today, it is a bit easier to get to the Barrier. In addition to Sea Bee Air, which operates from the Auckland Harbor, Great Barrier Airlines has daily scheduled service from either of two Auckland airports. Those who prefer to go by boat have a choice of a barge that goes out every Friday or a schooner that calls in once a month.

I'm not the only person who was impressed by this cheerful

Maori woman and her snowy-haired commercial-fisherman husband. These comments from her guest book are typical: "Enjoyed your company immensely"; "Food was five stars plus"; "Das essen ist wunderbar"; "My only regret is that we have to leave."

BRIAN BORU HOTEL

Pollen Street
Thames; (0843) 86-523
■

HOSTESS: Barbara Doyle.
LOCATION: Coromandel Peninsula, seventy-five miles southeast of Auckland.
CATEGORY: Historic hotel.
ACCOMMODATIONS: Twenty-two rooms, eleven with private bath.
RATES: Inexpensive.
INCLUDED: Room only.
CREDIT CARDS: All major.

Gold was discovered near Thames (pronounced "Tems," as in England) on the Coromandel Peninsula in the mid-1860s. At the height of the rush that resulted, 127 hotels were dispensing alcohol to thirsty miners. One of these hotels was the Brian Boru, built in 1868 by an immigrant from Ireland named Twohill who named his new establishment after an Irish folk hero.

The population of Thames, which swelled to 18,000 at the turn of the century, is now 6,500, and only five of the original 127 hotels remain. However, this picturesque little community is far from being a ghost town. On the contrary, its proximity to Auckland makes it a popular day trip for residents of that city when they seek a change of pace. It's also handy for overseas visitors with little time for exploring New Zealand.

I first heard about the Brian Boru from my host at a home stay in suburban Auckland. He had discovered it at the end of a camping trip on the Coromandel several months before and was still raving about the great meal he'd had in the hotel's dining room. Now that I've been there, I can say that his enthusiasm is justified.

Lunch and dinner are served seven days a week, and the menu includes quail braised in port wine sauce, scallops sautéed with cucumbers and cream, roast lamb with tamarillo and mint sauce, and quail eggs on spinach.

Many people come to the Brian Boru because they've heard about the great meals, but others are attracted by the old-world appearance of the hotel. Its charcoal gray weatherboard exterior is complemented by a white verandah and a cherry red iron roof.

The hotel and its guests are lovingly looked after by proprietor Barbara Doyle, who bought the Brian Boru from the Twohill family. There's no doubt that her success is due to hard work and a talent for making guests feel welcome. As she explained it, "Some people don't like being fussed over, but I'm good at fussing over people if they want it. Nothing they ask for is too much trouble."

Barbara learned about innkeeping at an early age. She was raised in Whitianga, farther north on the Coromandel Peninsula, where her father was a commercial fisherman and her mother ran a guest house. During World War II, most of their guests were U.S. servicemen.

Since taking over the Brian Boru, Barbara has renovated the bedrooms with private baths, and they are now "small, clean, and comfortable," to use her words. The rooms without private baths have yet to be redecorated.

She's also reinstituted traditional morning and afternoon teas, which are served in the dining room from nine to noon and from two to four every day.

Those who'd prefer something stronger than tea have a choice of two bars, both of which offer classic turn-of-the-century pub decor and friendly local people. As in all Kiwi public-licensed hotels, the public bar attracts workingmen, the lounge bar caters to couples and professional types, and both bars are closed on Sunday.

Visitors shouldn't be surprised if the locals in the pub talk about their "claims" and the new gold rush yet to come. Thames is ringed by rugged knolls, and the consensus of opinion around town is that there's gold in them there hills.

THE GOOD LIFE GUEST HOUSE

P.O. Box 10 Racecourse Road
Whitianga; (0843) 65-461

■

HOSTS: Ellinor and Jim Hawley.

LOCATION: Coromandel Peninsula, forty-two miles northeast of Thames.

CATEGORY: Bed and breakfast inn.

ACCOMMODATIONS: Six rooms, all with private bath.

RATES: Inexpensive.

INCLUDED: Breakfast.

CREDIT CARDS: None.

Jim and Ellinor Hawley did what many city dwellers dream of doing — they left the rat race behind and went to the countryside in search of the good life. And, after considerable hard work, they found it.

Jim decided to give up his stressful job in Auckland and move to Whitianga after a short vacation in the peaceful little seaside community. At the time he was middle-aged, facing major surgery, and coping with the metropolitan treadmill by taking tranquilizers. Ellinor, who is German, hadn't been in New Zealand very long.

The transition wasn't easy. The parcel of land they bought had potential for farming, but it was without a house in which to live. Slowly they built one, gradually buying construction supplies as the budget allowed. Everything was done with careful planning and with regard for the environment.

The Good Life Guest House, where they live and where others are welcome to share their enviable existence, is the end result.

What is the Hawleys' idea of the good life? To them it means no traffic, no city noise, time to communicate, classical music during dinner, fresh vegetables, tea made with rainwater, home-made bread, and no preservatives.

It also means independence, and signs of their self-reliance are everywhere: the down in the pillows comes from their geese and ducks; the sheepskins used for rugs were tanned by Jim; the bacon is from their pigs, the eggs from their chickens; Ellinor spins fleeces into yarn and knits their sweaters.

Guests who want to sample their way of life are accommodated in simply furnished, comfortable rooms with either one double or two twin beds. Dinner is available for an extra charge of about $5, and meals are eaten with the hosts, family-style.

"There is no television," Jim says, "because we're trying to prove that the art of conversation isn't dead." Each night after dinner he invites everyone into the living room and very informally gets the ball rolling.

If the time I spent with the Hawleys is typical, I can say with certainty that the art of conversation is alive and well, at least in Whitianga. First, Jim told us the story of how he and Ellinor met when they were both vacationing in Italy and how he courted her. It was a romantic tale, and soon others in the room were sharing their own stories.

For daytime activities, some guests go out on the farm, where there are milking cows, beef stock, sheep, milking goats, geese, rabbits, and other animals. Others walk down to Buffalo Beach or drive to one of the other forty-three white-sand beaches in the area. Cycling, boating, fishing, hiking, and flightseeing are popular in the area. The big-game fishing season extends from Christmas to the end of April.

And for Ellinor and Jim Hawley and their guests, the good life starts on Racecourse Road.

TEQUILA

71 Franklin Road
Freemans Bay, Auckland, (09) 769-185
■

HOSTS: Mollie and D'arcy Whiting.

LOCATION: At home at sea.

CATEGORY: Something different.

ACCOMMODATIONS: Six berths share one head.

RATES: Moderately expensive.

INCLUDED: All meals, wine with dinner, and thirty to forty miles of sailing per day.

CREDIT CARDS: None.

St. Ambrose counseled travelers, "When you are at Rome, live in the Roman style." Visitors who want to follow this advice in Auckland, where one in eight residents owns a pleasure boat of some sort, must also take to the water.

I can't think of a more pleasant way to do this than to join D'arcy and Mollie Whiting aboard their forty-six-foot racing sloop *Tequila*. Guests couldn't ask for better company with which to cruise the Hauraki Gulf and the Bay of Islands. D'arcy is a charming old salt from a prestigious New Zealand sailing family, and his first mate (in both senses), Mollie, is such a good cook that guests "have threatened to sue us for the weight they've gained."

D'arcy became a charter sailboat (yacht) skipper after an illustrious racing career. He sailed *Tequila* to admirable finishes in the Sydney-to-Hobart race, the Trans Tasman, the Suva Regatta, and the Auckland-to-Noumea race, to name just a few. He also spent three years sailing around the world with his family on board. Now enjoying his new role, he says, "As much as I love sailing, I also love the wonderful people I meet. It's a way of life and I like it very much."

His passengers are encouraged to help with the boat but don't need to have a great deal of experience. D'arcy teaches basic navigation skills at the same time as he introduces visitors to secluded beaches, sheltered harbors, and tiny islands that the vast majority of tourists will never see.

The Mimiwhangata Peninsula near the Bay of Islands is a good example. Queen Elizabeth II went there for lunch on her ship

Britannia in 1977 and liked it so much she stayed for two days. However, since there is no road access, very few people have ever seen the miles of golden-sand beaches this stretch of land offers.

No one is more capable than D'arcy — who is a co-author of *The Coastal Cruising Handbook* — of finding a picturesque anchorage where there are no other boats. However, sailing with this popular skipper can also be a very sociable experience, since he seems to have friends on every island and in every port in New Zealand. One place he likes to visit, the Kingfish Lodge at Whangaroa, can only be reached by boat. When *Tequila* calls in, hosts Carrie and Richard Barron welcome D'arcy and his friends with open arms.

When she isn't under sail, the sloop, which is named after her skipper's favorite beverage, is moored at Auckland's Westhaven Marina. She can be chartered for a minimum of two days and a maximum of two weeks. The rate is "moderately expensive" with a minimum of four people and "expensive" when there are only two passengers. The sailing season extends from October to June but is best from January to March.

D'arcy likes Americans because, among other reasons, "they return a shout in the pub." This has nothing to do with raising one's voice but instead refers to taking a turn at buying a round of drinks. It's a well-established Kiwi tradition that D'arcy, who concurs with St. Ambrose, thinks visitors should observe.

Northland

The region that stretches from the northern margin of the greater Auckland area to the extreme north end of the country is known as Northland. The mild climate, beautiful beaches, and available water sports found in this area make it one of the most popular parts of the nation.

The focal point of Northland is the Bay of Islands, which is composed of 150 islands and several small townships, including Russell, Waitangi, and Paihia. It was here that the first European settlements in New Zealand were established and the Treaty of Waitangi, in which Maori chiefs ceded sovereignty to Queen Victoria, was signed on February 6, 1840.

Because of its semitropical weather, Northland, which is sometimes known as "the winterless north," makes an especially good destination for people who visit New Zealand during the chilly June-to-September period. However, regardless of the time of year, no one should miss the Cape Reinga lighthouse and Ninety Mile Beach, two of New Zealand's most spectacular sights.

Warkworth is a good overnight stop for those wishing to tour Kawau Island; Dargaville is handy for visitors who want to explore the Waipoua Kauri Forest.

WARKWORTH ESTABLISHMENT

Queen Street
Warkworth, (0846) 8569

■

HOST: Dan Haydon.

LOCATION: Fifty miles north of Auckland.

CATEGORY: Historic hotel.

ACCOMMODATIONS: Eleven rooms, none with private bath.

RATES: Inexpensive.

INCLUDED: Room only.

CREDIT CARDS: All major.

For some reason, fish and chips always taste better in a country pub. I'm not sure if it's the atmosphere or the congenial company. On the other hand, it could also be the lager. Whatever it is, every visitor to New Zealand should have a pub lunch of fish and chips at least once, and the Warkworth Establishment would be a good place to do it.

The hotel was built in 1863 so that farmers in the surrounding area could have a drink when they came into town. In those days, it wasn't legal to build a bar (a "tavern license" is still relatively new in New Zealand). Alcohol could only be dispensed at a hotel. Although there was little intention that anyone would use them, accommodations had to be constructed to satisfy the licensing laws. In the case of the Warkworth Establishment, there are three bars and eleven bedrooms.

The lounge bar, with its wooden tables and brass rails, is popular for lunch. The hotel is owned by Lion Breweries, so their products—Lion Red, Lion Brown, and so forth—are on tap. New Zealanders distinguish between a beer, a draught, and a lager, and any of the locals can explain how these brews differ from one another.

In addition to the bistro meals served in the bar, lunch and dinner are also offered in the Silver Room Restaurant. In this lovely room, so named for the original silver serving pieces still in use, visitors can sample dishes that are unique to New Zealand. For instance, whitebait fritters are available as either a first course (entree) or an entrée (main course). These omelet-type patties are made of tiny transparent fish. Another first-course option is deep-fried Camembert cheese served with plum sauce. Both of these items are popular with Kiwis.

Those who are interested in staying overnight will find the six upstairs bedrooms that have been redecorated to be very comfortable. Each cheerful room has cane furniture, a sink, facilities for making tea and coffee, and a radio. High ceilings are all that belie the otherwise youthful appearance of the accommodations.

There's no traffic noise to disturb guests' sleep because Warkworth (pop. 1,600) is by-passed by Highway 1, the main north-south route. However, the daily intercity bus from Auckland makes the detour into town and stops near the two-story, cream-colored colonial hotel.

Many years ago, I took this bus from Auckland bound for Sandspit, where I was going to catch the ferry over to Kawau Island (Mansion House, the restored home of former governor Sir George Grey, is open daily). When the bus stopped in Warkworth, we had a few minutes to spare, and I ran into the hotel to get a cup of tea. Much to my dismay, the tea was unusually hot, and try as I did I couldn't get it cool enough to swallow. I was left with the choice of missing the bus or abandoning the tea.

If I'd been smart, I'd have ordered fish and chips — to go.

DUKE OF MARLBOROUGH HOTEL

The Strand, P.O. Box 52
Russell, (0885) 37-829
■

HOSTS: Raewyn and Karl Andersen.
LOCATION: Bay of Islands, 160 miles north of Auckland.
CATEGORY: Historic hotel.
ACCOMMODATIONS: Twenty-nine rooms, all with private bath.
RATES: Moderate.
INCLUDED: Room only.
CREDIT CARDS: All major.

On July 14, 1840, the Colonial Treasury issued the first hotel liquor license ever granted in the fledgling British territory of New

Zealand. The recipient of the license built his hotel in the settlement of Russell, which had been a regular port of call for sailing ships, mainly whalers, since the early 1800s and had just become the first capital of the new colony.

The original structure and the two that followed it were claimed by conflagrations and Maori war parties, but the present Duke of Marlborough Hotel, built in 1932, still holds that first license. The hotel is sited squarely on the waterfront, where it maintains its role as the center of Russell's social life.

The accommodations area of the hotel has been totally renovated. Today, every room has a private bath, a color television, coffee- and tea-making facilities, and the vivid chenille bedspreads that are so popular in New Zealand. The comfortable, front-facing rooms have telephones and a bird's-eye vista of harbor activities, including the ferry, which brings passengers to Russell from Paihia. A swimming pool and a sauna are available to guests.

Room six has a double bed and a twin and overlooks the harbor. Number seven, a spacious corner suite with an extra-wide view, seems to be the most popular. These are the quarters chosen by Queen Elizabeth II when she stayed at "the Duke" in 1954, by actor Mike Farrell ("M*A*S*H") when he came to Russell to tape a series of water safety messages for Television New Zealand in 1985, and by New Zealand's Governor General Reeves in 1986.

Downstairs, several huge mounted marlins and photos taken at game-fishing tournaments adorn the walls of the large guest lounge and bar. It's been a while since Zane Grey called this area "an angler's El Dorado," but the possibility of landing a swordfish, mako shark, or marlin is still what draws many people. The lounge, which has attractive cane furniture and huge picture windows, is a busy place during the best months for big-game fishing, January to May. During the winter (June to August), when a reduced room rate is in effect, locals and visitors gather around the fireplace and swap fish stories and general gossip.

The appealing exterior of the traditional colonial frame hotel suggests the old-world charm that contributes to the popularity of this hostelry. The friendly service, central location, sense of history, and waterfront views are other important factors.

It's not surprising that fresh seafood is featured on the lunch and dinner menus in the hotel's dining room. It's also offered nearby at the Gables Restaurant, which is considered to be

Russell's finest eatery. Either spot would be good for trying local snapper, lobster, oysters, or smoked marlin.

The Gables is housed in a homey waterfront cottage that, like the venerable Duke of Marlborough Hotel, has endured Russell's colorful history.

OKIATO LODGE

Old Russell Road
Okiato Point, R.D. 1 Russell; (0885) 37-948
■

HOSTS: Gina and Gary Kenny.
LOCATION: Bay of Islands, 160 miles north of Auckland.
CATEGORY: Country lodge.
ACCOMMODATIONS: Four junior suites, all with private bath.
RATES: Very expensive.
INCLUDED: All meals, wine with dinner, cocktails, sightseeing and boating.
CREDIT CARDS: All major.

I haven't learned many Maori words, probably because new Zealand's native people all speak English and a knowledge of their language isn't necessary for communication. However, there is one term I'll never forget, and that is *okiato*, which means "a place where precious objects are stored." This word became a permanent part of my vocabulary when I stayed at Okiato Lodge near Russell, because when I was there I noticed that guests are treated with the same TLC one gives to very special objets d'art. In fact, the lodge was named after the point of land on which it was built, but there couldn't be a more appropriate title for an inn where VIP service is standard.

Guests who arrive by air are greeted at either the Sea Bee Air Terminal in Paihia or the Kerikeri Airport, which is served by Mount Cook Airline. It's also possible to drive to Okiato Point using the car ferry from Opua. In either case, the travel-weary are usually greatly relieved by their first glimpse of the lodge.

The multilevel structure was designed by Greg Vindriis, a Danish architect now living in New Zealand, and constructed of

Okiato Lodge

radiata pine. It is set in native woodland and surrounded by water on two sides.

The interior features a large, elegantly furnished living room with cathedral-style open-beam ceilings and a fireplace. The spacious bedrooms are decorated with Danish modern furniture made of rimu wood and are illuminated by both a skylight and attractive brass and glass chandeliers. Each room has two beds, a queen and a twin, and a sunken sitting area with water view. There's also a skylight in the bathroom.

Outside, a hot tub and lounge chairs are provided on wooden decks that overlook Pipiroa Bay to one side and the Veronica Channel to the other. Gina and Gary are outdoorsy people and encourage their guests to join them on the patio for breakfast and lunch when the weather is right.

All meals are prepared by the lodge chef, David Christie, who came to Okiato when it opened in 1986. He was formerly the chef at Huka Lodge (described in the next chapter), which is world-renowned for its gourmet fare.

David's recipes and talent make every meal at Okiato Lodge an event to be remembered. For one al fresco lunch he served a delicious soup made of puréed spinach and walnut pieces. This was followed by seafood crepes and accompanied by a good white pinot noir.

I wondered why Gina referred to this noble repast as "casual," but I understood that evening when I encountered one of David's formal five-course gourmet dinners.

We started with a heart-shaped smoked-eel mousse, drizzled with asparagus sauce and garnished with caviar. This was followed by wild boar and thyme soup served with a glass of medium dry sherry, which we were given the choice of drinking or adding to the soup. Cascade Creek whitebait tossed in flour and pan-fried in butter preceded the main course, breast of pheasant. Snow eggs, soft meringues flavored with apricot brandy, were served for dessert. Everything was superb. (The Kennys offer a less expensive, room-only tariff for calorie-conscious travelers.)

I especially enjoyed Gina and Gary's company. After the meal, we moved into their gorgeous living room, where we shared some good port, listened to music, and talked until the wee hours.

The next day, some guests were anxious to go out on Gary's twenty-two-foot cabin cruiser. The plan was to do some bottom fishing and have a picnic lunch on board.

The rest of us elected to remain in the okiato.

TITORE WAY

P.O. Box 60
Russell, (0885) 37-658

■

HOSTS: Diana and Morrell Folley.
LOCATION: Bay of Islands, 160 miles north of Auckland.
CATEGORY: Home stay.
ACCOMMODATIONS: Two rooms, none with private bath.
RATES: Moderate.
INCLUDED: All meals, wine with dinner.
CREDIT CARDS: All major.

If the comments in their guest book are any indication, Diana and Morrell Folley have never had an unsatisfied customer. One American woman called it, "One hundred percent better than the Auckland hotel I paid a fortune for." Another summed up her feelings with "Making new friends in such a beautiful place is what I'd hoped my vacation would be."

It's very easy to see why the Folleys' home on Titore Way would be popular with overseas visitors. Diana and Morrell are warm, caring people who go out of their way to see that their guests make the most of their time in Russell. They take people sightseeing if they don't have their own car and help them decide which day tours they would most enjoy.

The Cape Reinga tour to the lighthouse at the tip of the North Island is a must, to be followed by the Cream Trip, the Hole-in-the-Rock Cruise, or the Tiger Lily.

Back when the Royal Mail went by stagecoach over land, Alfred Fuller was appointed to carry the post by boat to isolated settlers in the Bay of Islands. Today, the boats on Fuller's Cream Trip still fly the Royal Mail flag, but the emphasis has shifted to showing off the scenery.

Russell is a quiet little town, pleasant for browsing. The main attractions are the Visitor Centre, where audio-visual displays tell about the early life of the community, and the Captain Cook Museum, which houses a twenty-two-foot replica of the *Endeavour*. This ship is the one in which Cook rediscovered New Zealand in 1769. (Abel Tasman sighted it first in 1642.) Titore Way is about a mile from the center of Russell, but the Folleys happily provide transportation both ways.

They also provide visitors with hearty bacon-and-egg breakfasts, light lunches, and three-course dinners. In addition, anyone can go in the kitchen and make tea and coffee at any time.

Meals are served near a big picture window, from which there is an expansive view of the Pacific Ocean and just a few of the 150 islands that dot the bay. The house is only several years old and is nicely furnished. One of the two cozy guest bedrooms, the one with the double bed, also has a water outlook. The bathroom is shared with the hosts.

Morrell Folley is a retired restaurateur who devotes himself full-time to the needs of overseas travelers. In response to his guests' requests for similar accommodations in other parts of New Zealand, he has gathered information about available hospitality and formed New Zealand Host Homes Ltd. (see the Appendix). Now he can help visitors plan the rest of their trip and book them into home stays along the way.

Diana is interested in gardening, sewing, spinning, and both machine and hand knitting. She has her own spinning wheel and will happily demonstrate for anyone who's interested. She also likes to cook, and after I took a look at her twenty-one-pound behemoth cat, I decided I couldn't afford — calorie-wise — to make this an extensive stay.

ABBA VILLA

21 School Road, P.O. Box 105
Paihia, (0885) 28-066

■

HOSTS: Vicky and Barrie Purves.
LOCATION: Bay of Islands, 160 miles north of Auckland.
CATEGORY: Bed and breakfast inn.
ACCOMMODATIONS: Seven rooms, none with private bath.
RATES: Inexpensive.
INCLUDED: Breakfast.
CREDIT CARDS: None.
RESTRICTIONS: No smoking.

It took Barrie Purves a while to convince me that Abba Villa wasn't brand-new. I assumed from the spotless carpeting and immaculate furnishings that this B & B had just recently opened. The five downstairs and two upstairs bedrooms have pretty floral wallpaper and sunny windows; the upper rooms also have cozy slanted ceilings. Two bathrooms are shared by guests, and a couple of the bedrooms have sinks.

The attractive parlor (guest lounge) has cane furniture, a television, a radio, facilities for making coffee and tea, and a refrigerator, which the hosts keep stocked with rainwater for drinking. They also see that plenty of reading material is available.

Barrie, who is a plumbing and drainage contractor, started working on his bed and breakfast inn several years ago while he was single-handedly raising his sons. The three of them lived on the premises in an older house, and when he finished the guest accommodation in 1982, it seemed appropriate to call it Abba Villa because *abba* means "father" in Hebrew.

In the meantime, Barrie went on a vacation to the Philippines, where he met Vicky and convinced her to leave her job at Texas Instruments and be his co-host in Paihia. She's still very interested in computers and enjoys talking to guests who work in her field.

The Purveses have a strong affection for the nearby kauri forest and drive interested visitors out to see it. They charge about $4 to cover expenses for the round trip, which takes an hour in their station wagon. Time is allowed for a short walk, which Barrie hopes "will give an appreciation of the lush New Zealand forest."

Abba Villa is well situated for travelers who don't have their own car. The major water excursions (Cream Trip, Tiger Lily, etc.) and the passenger ferry to Russell leave from the main wharf, a five-minute walk away. With prior arrangement, all motorized local tours pick up at the inn. In addition, Barrie and Vicky will collect guests who arrive in Paihia by bus.

The Waitangi Treaty House is less than a mile and a half down the road. The Visitor Center at the Treaty House, officially opened by Prince Charles in 1983, contains excellent displays and a very good film about early New Zealand history.

The central location of Abba Villa also makes it convenient for guests to walk to a variety of restaurants. The Bella Vista is known for its seafood, and the Courtyard is a popular BYO. Both dining spots have water views; in the busy season they require reservations ahead of time.

According to Barrie, one of New Zealand's best eighteen-hole golf courses is the one located near the Visitor Center at Waitangi. When guests want to try it, he loans them clubs.

He also makes dinner reservations, sees that his house guests eat a good breakfast, and teaches people how to fish.

Just like a father.

Aspley House

ASPLEY HOUSE

Atkinson's Road, Ohaeawai R. D.
Waimate North, OW 424

■

HOSTS: Joy and Frank Atkinson.

LOCATION: Central Bay of Islands, ten miles west of Paihia.

CATEGORY: Farm stay.

ACCOMMODATIONS: Two rooms share one bath.

RATES: Moderate.

INCLUDED: All meals, wine with dinner.

CREDIT CARDS: None.

RESTRICTIONS: No children.

Visitors who stay with Joy and Frank Atkinson get a bonus. In addition to enjoying the company of two very nice people, guests at Aspley House also have the advantage of learning about local history from a man who is descended from one of New Zealand's first colonists.

Instead of visiting the nearby Waimate Mission House on a hurried bus tour, the Atkinsons' house guests can roam the grounds and hear personalized history from a couple whose ancestors are buried in the adjoining churchyard. And later, over afternoon tea in their living room, Frank will happily expand on the human stories that give meaning to the early settlement of the country.

The Mission House, the only remaining building of New Zealand's first inland mission station, was built from 1831 to 1832. Its creators wanted to teach the local Maoris efficient farming techniques at the same time as they gave religious instruction. For a time, the mission thrived. In 1835 visiting naturalist Charles Darwin wrote, "After having passed over so many miles of un-inhabited useless country, the sudden appearance of an English farmhouse and its well-dressed fields . . . was exceedingly pleasing."

Today, the house, which contains an interesting collection of missionary items, is administered by the Historic Places Trust.

One item of historic interest that isn't stored in the Mission House is the marble plaque that Frank's great-grandfather carried with him when he left Aspley, Yorkshire, England, in 1860. Inscribed with the words "Aspley House," the plaque now stands by the Atkinsons' front door. This relative and others brought out the Scottish furniture, which lends an old-world atmosphere to the new-world Aspley House.

These antiques contribute to the charm of the two large, twin-bedded rooms available to guests. Both of these have French doors that open onto a verandah overlooking the surrounding lush farmland. The modern bathroom is shared by the occupants of the two bedrooms but not by the hosts.

When they aren't soaking up local history or taking in Bay of Islands activities, the Atkinsons' visitors go out on the tractor with Frank across some of the 750 acres where he runs Hereford cattle and Romney sheep. Most people just watch farm activities, but some get more involved. One male house guest was recruited to help pull a cow out of a stream; a woman who was visiting at shearing time took home a fleece to spin into knitting yarn.

Sometimes one of the Atkinsons' daughters, who is a horticul-turist, stops off to visit her parents and gives impromptu tours of their orchard. At other times visitors just laze around the swimming pool and catch up on postcards.

Whatever their daytime activities, everyone looks forward to the evening meal. The highlight of these three-course dinners is dessert, when guests get to sample homemade English trifle, boiled pudding, fresh fruit salad, or cheesecake. Joy often serves two sweets on the same night and encourages everyone to have some of each.

These delicious second helpings, like the personalized history lessons, are an Aspley House bonus.

KAURI HOUSE LODGE

Bowen Street
Dargaville, (0884) 8082
■

HOSTS: June and Doug Blaxall
LOCATION: One hundred eleven miles northwest of Auckland.
CATEGORY: Bed and breakfast inn.
ACCOMMODATIONS: Three rooms, all with private bath.
RATES: Moderate.
INCLUDED: Room only.
CREDIT CARDS: None.

Travelers who have wondered, as they toured a historic house, what it would be like to stay there — especially those who have felt the urge to step over the gold cord barring the entrance to a room full of elegant furniture and climb into bed — need wonder no more. The Kauri House Lodge, which contains some of the most interesting antique kauri furniture in New Zealand, accepts overnight guests.

Visitors have a choice of three bedrooms, two with double beds and one with twins. Each is chock-a-block (chocka) with headboards, washstands, and dressers made of the attractive native New Zealand timber.

The five-thousand-square-foot house was built by C. J. Carrington, a master builder who later became a member of the Legislative Council. He began construction in 1910 and finished in 1914. The colonial-style exterior, including a wide verandah, is made of kauri and painted white. Under the green iron roof, eighteen spacious rooms have twelve-foot ceilings that, like the walls, are covered in kauri paneling.

The most striking interior feature is an eighty-foot hallway with large stained-glass windows in foyers at either end. The ceiling in this area is made of pressed zinc, and bedroom doors opening onto the passageway are inset with panels of rare mottled kauri.

At first glance, some of the furniture appears to be mahogany. This is because it was made by English craftsmen who had just come to New Zealand and felt that pieces made of local timber would be considered inferior. To add worth to their work, they created in the classic Victorian style and stained the wood to look like mahogany. The huge antique sideboard in the dining room was treated this way, but the ten-foot kauri dining room table was left in its natural shade.

It is around this table that guests gather with the Blaxalls and their two teen-agers for breakfast and dinner. (Meals aren't included in the tariff, but breakfast is available for an extra $2-4, and dinner costs about $6.) In the evening, assorted main courses and side dishes are passed around family-style, and the hosts generously supply a glass of wine to those who wish it.

It was hard for me to adjust to the idea that this museum of antique furniture was also a private home. Not only are there no gold cords across the bedroom doorways, but the billiard room, drawing room, and library are actively used by the Blaxalls and their children and guests. An amazing collection of Victorian bric-a-brac fills these rooms, along with modern-day trappings like televisions and stereos.

June and Doug immigrated from England in 1965. After buying the lodge in 1973, they set about restoring it and replacing furniture that had been sold. Today, Doug owns a second-hand shop in Dargaville, and June concentrates on their garden, which boasts five hundred to six hundred dahlias of various sizes and colors. They sometimes exhibit the flowers during the January-to-April blooming period.

Kauri House Lodge is set at the end of a long driveway in eight acres of flowers, trees, and pasture. Doug says staying with them is "just like staying with a family, but you get a bill before you leave."

But I bet most guests think of it as the only time they were ever allowed to sleep in a museum.

Auckland to Wellington

Only four hundred miles separate the two major North Island cities, Auckland and Wellington. This distance could easily be covered in a day, but the savvy traveler will take a week or more to do it. Without this additional time, some of New Zealand's best scenery and most interesting sights will be by-passed.

For instance, it would be a shame to miss Cambridge, nestled in the lush green Waikato region, known for its highly productive farming and successful horse studs. The town is a center for antiques, and several stores are located within a few blocks of each other.

Mount Maunganui, on the Bay of Plenty, has one of the nicest beaches in New Zealand and is a good area for big-game fishing.

The heart of the Maori culture and dramatic thermal activity are both to be found in Rotorua. Taupo is known for trout fishing; Wanganui is a picturesque riverside city as yet undiscovered by the majority of tourists.

Mount Egmont is a nearly perfect symmetrical cone, often compared to Japan's Fujiyama. It is this eight-thousand-foot peak that causes the North Island to bulge about two-thirds of the way down the west coast.

Marton, named after Captain James Cook's English birthplace, services an area of intensive sheep farming. Palmerston North is the home of Massey University. Masterton is the center of the wealthy Wairarapa ("Wy-ra-pa") agricultural district.

Unfortunately, the trend is for New Zealand's first-time visitors to land in Auckland, drive south to the Waitomo Glow-worm Grotto, and continue on to much-publicized attractions in Rotorua. I wouldn't for a minute suggest that these sights should be skipped, but I would hope that every itinerary would also allow time to pause with a farming family in a rural area. And I hope that there would be time for a walk — whether beside the river in Wanganui, through the antique stores in Cambridge, along the beach at Mount Manganui, or to the top of Mount Egmont.

PARK HOUSE

70 Queen Street, Victoria Square
Cambridge; (7127) 6368

■

HOSTS: Pat and Bill Hargreaves.

LOCATION: Ninety-five miles southeast of Auckland.

CATEGORY: Home stay.

ACCOMMODATIONS: Four rooms, two with private bath.

RATES: Moderate.

INCLUDED: Breakfast, dinner, and wine with dinner.

CREDIT CARDS: All major.

It's hard to imagine what Park House must have looked like when the Hargreaveses purchased it in 1978. According to Pat and Bill, the original structure was built in 1925 and used as a private boarding house. Later, it became an inn with a five-star rating, but the stars were lost at the rate of about one per decade. By the time the Hargreaveses rescued it, things were in a sad state of repair.

However, if they had told me the elegant Georgian mansion had always been their family home, I would have believed them because not even the tiniest hint of neglect is evident today.

The property, which is bordered by a lich gate similar to those found on the perimeters of English churchyards, is entered via a circular drive. Guests are greeted in the foyer, where squares of black and white marble form a checkerboard pattern. The doors opening onto this hallway have panels of beveled glass, and the area is illuminated by a crystal chandelier.

Throughout the house a combination of New Zealand and English antiques; tastefully coordinated draperies, upholstery, and wall colors; and stained-glass windows creates a stately atmosphere.

The guest wing upstairs offers a choice of three rooms. The one with two twin beds and the one with one twin share a bathroom; the double room has its own bath and a view of the tree-lined village park across the street. Another double downstairs also has an attached bath. Each of the bedrooms is decorated with antiques, including brass headboards and mahogany towel racks. One large bathroom sports a claw-foot tub and gleaming brass fittings.

The well-appointed decor is matched by Pat and Bill's caring attitude toward their guests. They've toured overseas a great deal and understand the needs of visitors. Coffee and tea facilities, complete with Royal Doulton china, are available in the guest wing for early risers. Picnic lunches are prepared for all-day outings. Extra bathrobes are kept on hand for the forgetful. And, while companionship and good conversation are always available, the hosts respect the travelers' need for privacy.

Park House cuisine includes homemade grapefruit marmalade and perked coffee at breakfast and creative beef and lamb dishes at dinner. On one recent evening a boned leg of lamb with blueberry sauce was accompanied by a molded broccoli ring and sautéed mushrooms. A gateau with raspberry purée was served for dessert.

The Hargreaveses enjoy inviting friends who share their guests' interests to dinner. This gives visitors a chance to meet more local people and talk about their favorite sport or hobby. When they aren't at boarding school, Pat and Bill's two teen-age daughters also join in these evening-meal discussions.

During the day, there are horse studs and dairy farms to visit and antique stores for browsing. Within walking distance of Park House, the Craft Centre offers an excellent selection of quality New Zealand handicrafts. The Waitomo Glow-worm Grotto is an hour's drive to the south, and Bay of Plenty beaches are the same distance north. In addition, the Hargreaveses invite house guests to use their hot tub and solar-heated swimming pool and will help to arrange games of tennis, squash, or golf on request.

I wasn't around fifty years ago when Park House was an inn with a five-star rating, but I'd be willing to bet it didn't offer the gracious hospitality and regal surroundings that are available now to guests who opt for a home stay with the Hargreaveses.

TAMATAKOI FARM

Puahue, R.D. 1
Te Awamutu, (082) 21-704
∎

HOSTS: Josephine and Vic Richards.

LOCATION: Ten miles from Cambridge.

CATEGORY: Farm stay.

ACCOMMODATIONS: Two rooms, each with private bath.

RATES: Moderate.

INCLUDED: All meals, wine with dinner.

CREDIT CARDS: All major.

I can't imagine anything more pleasant than sleeping in the Richardses' twin-bedded guest room and awakening to their classic New Zealand travel-poster view of rolling green hills dotted with sheep. Farms in the Waikato region are more lush and hilly than in other parts of the country, and theirs is one of the nicest.

Jo and Vic own 850 acres, on which they run three thousand sheep, two hundred Friesian cattle, and a small herd of goats. They also grow blackberries, boysenberries, and maize. Vic takes guests around the property in a four-wheel-drive vehicle, and visitors can either observe or participate in the care of the animals. Part of his farm tour includes a chance for their sheep dog to show off his talent. The dog's a real ham and seems to thoroughly enjoy having an appreciative audience.

The other guest room has a double bed and a view of the large, colorful country garden that surrounds the house. Camellias, tamarillos, passionflowers, and papaya (pawpaw) grow on all sides of the attractive white colonial-style home which was built in the 1930s. Naturally, the flowers are at their best in the summer, and that is also when the swimming pool, tennis court, and barbecue area get the most use.

Jo and Vic are recreation-oriented people, and, except for the formal drawing room, their house is casual and comfortable. Jo tells guests to make themselves at home in her large blue-and-white tile kitchen, and she means it. The Ping-Pong table in the rumpus room and the billiard table in another room provide indoor diversions.

Outdoor pursuits include golf, walks through native woodland, and turkey shooting. Vic also enjoys windsurfing and sailing, and with advance planning a trip aboard their thirty-five-foot sailboat moored in Auckland can be arranged.

Jo's hobbies include making wine, spinning, making porcelain dolls, and windsurfing. Their teen-age son Stuart shares his parents' enthusiasm for home hosting and, like them, goes out of his way to see that visitors have a good time.

The Richardses' property is conveniently located a short drive from the Maori carving center in Te Awamutu and only forty-five minutes from the Waitomo Glow-worm Grotto.

The caves at Waitomo are one of New Zealand's major tourist attractions. Carved out of limestone hills by underground streams over many thousands of years, the caverns are the dwelling place of thousands of tiny glowworms that sparkle in the darkness. Their twinkling light creates a fairytale beauty that really must be seen to be believed. Stalactites, stalagmites, and intricate limestone pillars add further interest. Visitors can make short excursions through the Glow-worm Grotto on foot and in boats.

The proximity to Waitomo is convenient, but the biggest advantage of staying at Tamatakoi Farm is a chance to savor warm Kiwi hospitality — and to wake up to the view of rolling green hills dotted with sheep.

MOOSE LODGE

R.D. 4
Rotorua, (073) 27-823
■

HOSTS: Noeline and Errol Officer.
LOCATION: Outside Rotorua on Lake Rotoiti.
CATEGORY: Country lodge.
ACCOMMODATIONS: Eight rooms, all with private bath.
RATES: Expensive.
INCLUDED: All meals and boating.
CREDIT CARDS: All major.

It's hard to write about Moose Lodge without using a liberal dose of flattering adjectives. Words like *breathtaking, superb, fabulous,* and *exquisite* are required to accurately describe this unusual country lodge and its elevated setting above the edge of Lake Rotoiti.

The seventeen-room mansion was built at the end of the 1930s by British-born Sir Noel Cole, a wealthy construction-industry magnate. He and his wife used the house for entertaining (Lady Cole referred to it as their "reception house") so that their home in Auckland could be kept very private. In 1954 Queen Elizabeth II and Prince Philip were guests at Moose Lodge. Sixteen years later, Prince Charles and Princess Anne followed their parents' lead. In addition, prime ministers from throughout the Commonwealth, leaders of international industry, and well-known theater personalities enjoyed the Coles' hospitality.

After Sir Noel died in 1976, the house was sold, but it remained a private holiday home until 1984. At that time, it was purchased by Auckland financier Errol Officer and his wife Noeline. They restored the mansion to its original grandeur and opened it to the public in April 1985.

In terms of the American experience, this is roughly equivalent to buying Walter Annenberg's Palm Springs estate — another spot to which British royalty regularly retreat — and turning it into an exclusive resort.

The Officers have handled the transition from private to public with good taste and decorum; the house still feels like the grand English home it was designed to resemble. In the living room a large picture window frames an expansive view of Lake Rotoiti, and quality furnishings, imported porcelain figurines, silver compotes, original oil paintings, and hand-painted china create a sense of elegance.

Queen Elizabeth slept in the twin-bedded green room; Prince Philip occupied the adjacent blue one. One suite has a four-poster canopy bed and a fabulous lake view. Honeymooners usually request the room downstairs that has a king bed, a huge spa bath, and another picture postcard vista.

The dining room, where cordon bleu cookery is served three times a day, accommodates five kauri tables; comfortable cane furniture in the sunlit breakfast niche encourages lingering over a second cup of coffee. The wine cellar is across from the billiard room.

Because it was designed with visiting heads of state in mind, the lodge is secluded on eighteen acres of grounds, and iron gates guard the entrance to the long, winding drive. In back of the house on the edge of the lake a group of Maori-style buildings shelter a large thermal pool, changing rooms, and a barbecue area.

Enthusiastic guests often sit in the hot pool and then run down a nearby dock and dive into the icy lake. Less energetic visitors prefer to cruise Rotoiti on the Officers' cocktail boat. A jet boat, a sailing dinghy, a canoe, and a cabin cruiser are also available.

Fisherman and hunters can be picked up by floatplane or helicopter and transported from Moose Lodge to other lakes or stalking grounds. Noeline and Errol collect their guests from the airport and accompany them on sightseeing excursions, picnics, or winery visits. Rotorua, with its thermal activity and Maori village, is only twelve miles down the road.

The Officers spend a lot of time determining what their visitors are interested in and making arrangements for them. As Noeline told me, "We try very hard to make everything exactly right, but it's a challenge because the people who come here have been everywhere and done everything else."

And she wasn't exaggerating. A list of recent guests included the names Robert Mitchum and Chuck Yeager.

PRINCE'S GATE HOTEL

P.O. Box 112, 1 Arawa Street
Rotorua, (073) 81-179
■

HOSTS: Diana and Keith McInerney.
LOCATION: Central Rotorua.
CATEGORY: Historic hotel.
ACCOMMODATIONS: Thirty-seven rooms, twenty-two with private bath.
RATES: Moderate.
INCLUDED: Breakfast.
CREDIT CARDS: All major.

The Prince's Gate is a breath of fresh air in a town where chain motels line the streets and modern brand-name hotels stand out on the skyline. In contrast, the two-story white colonial with its wide verandahs and blue iron roof projects an old-world atmosphere from a choice corner location adjacent to the en-

Prince's Gate

trance of Government Gardens. The New Zealand Tourist and Publicity Office — the best source for local sightseeing information — and the major shops and restaurants are all within a few blocks.

For me, the hotel was a case of love at first sight. I was attracted by the lacy timber fretwork used to decorate the peaks and support posts of the verandahs, by the stained-glass windows, and by the surrounding stately garden of ferns. These elements enhance the old gem's inherent Victorian charm.

Inside, a kauri staircase with hand-carved balustrade leads up to bedrooms decorated in pink, green, or mauve, with private baths. Fluffy comforters, pretty floral wallpaper, and color-coordinated sheets and curtains are a cheerful sight. One delightful room even has a big bathtub set on gilded feet. Unlike the nonfacilitied quarters, these rooms have televisions and supplies for making coffee and tea.

Until I talked to Keith and Diana, I assumed that the historic hostelry had been built on its present site and that Rotorua (pop. 50,000) had grown up around it. However, I learned from the McInerneys that the Prince's Gate was constructed in Waihi (ninty-five miles to the north) in 1899 and was a popular spot there until 1909, when the townsfolk voted in prohibition and all the pubs were closed. After that, the building sat idle until 1919, when someone decided it should be moved to Rotorua. As a result, the hotel was dismantled board by board, each piece was numbered, and the Prince's Gate was transported by bullock cart to its new home, where it once again became a favorite watering hole. During World War II, it was used by the air force as a recuperation center.

Keith and Diana said that it's not unusual for men who rested in Rotorua during the war years to come back for a return stay. However, most guests are overseas visitors attracted by the hotel's central location, inviting appearance, and friendly management.

Keith dispenses advice on local attractions while he tends the cozy bar. Diana and her cat Cheeky hold forth in the adjacent television lounge, where they greet everyone coming and going. Guests are welcome to use the attractive thermal pool at the rear of the hotel.

A cooked breakfast is included in the room rate, and four-course dinners are available for an extra charge of about $7. The entrée of these dinners is usually roast lamb, beef, or pork.

These home-style meals, like the hotel itself, offer a pleasant change for travelers who are tired of traditional tourist fare.

EATON HALL

39 *Hinemaru Street*
Rotorua, (073) 70-366
■

HOSTS: Pat and Clive King.

LOCATION: Central Rotorua.

CATEGORY: Bed and breakfast inn.

ACCOMMODATIONS: Eight rooms, one with private bath.

RATES: Inexpensive.

INCLUDED: Breakfast.

CREDIT CARDS: All major.

Even before I met Pat and Clive King, I suspected that the owners of Eaton Hall were not native New Zealanders. The B & B has an unmistakably British feel to it. The upholstery in the living room is English chintz, and the dark green color scheme isn't one that Kiwis would have chosen.

When I heard their accents, my suspicions were confirmed. Pat is Scottish-Irish and Clive is English. When they immigrated to New Zealand in 1972, they hoped to be able to open an English-style bed and breakfast inn. Eaton Hall is the happy result of those dreams.

The two-story, sixty-year-old inn sits in an ideal location near Government Gardens and only a couple of short blocks from the main street of Rotorua. In the Gardens, visitors can use the thermal Polynesian Pools or attend a Maori concert party at Tudor Towers. There's also an orchid display in a large greenhouse (glasshouse), a croquet lawn, a bowling green, and a rose garden.

A Continental breakfast is included in the tariff at Eaton Hall, but hearty eaters who want a full English-style menu need only pay an extra $2. Clive's baked beans on toast, spaghetti on toast, and bacon-and-egg repasts are so popular that guests from the Hyatt Kingsgate Hotel across the street often come to this bed and breakfast inn for their morning meal. (The rooms at the Hyatt cost six times the tariff at Eaton Hall, and the B & B offers a reduced rate during the quieter winter months.)

It's not surprising that dinners, which are available for an additional $6, feature roast beef and Yorkshire pudding, cauliflower with cheese sauce, and other British dishes.

The inn's bedrooms are spacious and cheerful, and each has its own sink. Because of the way the house is designed, the attractive sleeping quarters have the feel of being part of a big family home. Coffee and tea facilities are provided in the upstairs hallway.

This same relaxed atmosphere prevails downstairs in the cozy living room, where it wouldn't be surprising to see a guest sprawled out on the floor watching television.

Next door to Eaton Hall, a delightful little deli called Potpourri sells quiche, meat pies, and filled croissants for lunch and imported cheeses, French bread, and cold cuts for those making up a picnic.

A few blocks away on Tutanekai Street, Continental fare is also served at the Gazebo Restaurant. Actually, the food is regional, but the approach is European: wonderful sauces and vegetables, checkered tablecloths, and outside tables when the weather permits.

Because Pat works for a company that sells wine and liquor to restaurants, she's up-to-date on the new spots in town and happily dispenses dining advice.

Both Pat and Clive enjoy sitting around talking to their guests and are very eager to be helpful. If they ever had any of the so-called British reserve, they've definitely traded it for the friendly Kiwi manner.

MORIHANA GUEST HOUSE

20 Toko Street
Rotorua, (073) 88-511
■

HOSTS: Sheila and Syd Saysell, Peter Johnson.
LOCATION: Central Rotorua.
CATEGORY: Bed and breakfast inn.
ACCOMMODATIONS: Eight rooms, none with private bath.
RATES: Inexpensive.
INCLUDED: Breakfast.
CREDIT CARDS: None.

If Sheila Saysell ever decides to leave the B & B business, I'm sure she could get a job with Rotorua's public relations office. This bubbly lady is a virtual font of visitor information, and she seems to take unusual pride in helping people organize their sightseeing. It's no wonder that some recent guests came for two days and stayed for twenty. I'm sure Sheila kept them busy the whole time.

Next to the front door of her guest house, a table is spread with brochures describing the myriad Rotorua activities. As Sheila explains it, "The attractions are basically of three types: those that feature the Maori culture, those that focus on thermal activity, and those that capitalize on the local springs."

For Maori culture she suggests a visit to the Whakarewarewa, where a model pa (a fortified village like the ones built before Europeans came to New Zealand) can be toured. The "Whaka" is also an area of great thermal activity: mud pools bubble constantly, and geysers explode with great regularity.

Sheila agrees with me that the best Maori concert party is the one at the THC Rotorua International, although these song and dance performances are given at most of the big hotels and at Tudor Towers in Government Gardens.

Regular bus tours carry visitors to thermal districts outside

Rotorua. Hell's Gate, Waimangu Valley, and Orakei Korako Geyserland are just three of these. Trips also go to Rainbow and Fairy Springs, Taniwha Springs, and Paradise Valley.

Above the table spread with brochures is a bulletin board on which Sheila has posted some of the thank-you notes she's received from all over the world. Almost everyone mentions how much they appreciate her valuable sightseeing advice.

After a day of touring, guests at the Morihana are happy to return to a quiet residential neighborhood, and no one seems to mind that the B & B is a ten-minute walk from the center of town. Most people choose to soak their weary bodies in the Saysells' attractive indoor thermal pool or have a cup of tea with Peter Johnson, Sheila's resident manager.

Peter lives on the premises and is available for friendly conversation or to answer questions after Sheila goes home in the afternoon. He's a great cribbage player and takes pleasure in routinely defeating any house guests he can lure into a game.

The bedrooms at the Morihana are comfortable, and each one has its own coffee and tea facilities. The inn's homey atmosphere stems from Peter and Sheila's caring attitude toward their visitors.

Breakfast is the only meal served at the B & B, but restaurants of all types abound in the area. Sheila recommends the Fenton Tavern, a nearby self-serve carvery (a cafeteria where hot meats are carved for customers as they go through the line) with entertainment. I like the Bamboo Garden for Cantonese, Aorangi Peak for fancy dining with a view, and the Tudor Cottage Bakery for take-out (takeaway) sandwiches.

However, for visitors who want something other than self-serve, Chinese, fancy, or take-out, I'm sure Sheila has lots of additional suggestions.

SOLITAIRE LODGE

R.D. 5
Rotorua, (073) 28-208
■

HOST: Reg Turner.

LOCATION: Outside Rotorua on Lake Tarawera.

CATEGORY: Country lodge.

ACCOMMODATIONS: Six rooms and one suite, each with private bath.

RATES: Very expensive.

INCLUDED: All meals, cocktails, wine with dinner, and boating.

CREDIT CARDS: All major.

RESTRICTIONS: No children under thirteen.

Trout fishing. That's what Solitaire Lodge is all about. Sure, the accommodations are comfortable, the meals are good, and the setting is idyllic, but what draw people to Reg Turner's lodge are rainbow trout — great big rainbow trout.

Some say that Lake Tarawera yields more trophy-sized fish than anywhere else in the hemisphere; if this is true, Reg is at least partly responsible. He seems to know where they hide and when and how to catch them off guard. And he loves a dramatic photo finish. Just when it seems a fisherman is going to go away empty-handed, Reg manages to guide him to the trout of his dreams.

This happened recently to the president of a major American oil company and his wife, whom I met over dinner at Solitaire on their last night in New Zealand. His heart's desire was to catch a trout, but after a full day in the boat with Reg he'd come back with nothing more than some good jokes to tell his friends in Chicago. Reg didn't seem worried; he knew they still had an hour in the morning before the couple's flight left Rotorua.

The next day, forty-seven minutes after Reg and his guest started across the lake in a boat, they were back — eight-and-a-half-pound rainbow trout in hand. The grinning executive quickly joined his wife in a waiting limousine, and the two were whisked off to the airport. His heart's desire was on ice in the trunk.

Solitaire is also popular with hunters, golfers, waterskiers, sailors, and hikers. There are several good golf courses in the area; one of Reg's boats can be used for waterskiing, another for sailing; helicopters ferry shooters to a variety of game.

Other guests prefer to let the lodge motto, *Dolce far niente*, it's sweet to do nothing, be their guide. The solitude and beauty of the lake invite contemplation, quiet strolls through surrounding native bushland, and long, lazy afternoon naps. If anyone is having trouble unwinding (highly unlikely), Reg suggests they go soak in the hot tub.

At dinner time, everyone compares notes on the day's activities. Nonfishing wives frequently make the thirty-minute trip to Rotorua for shopping or sightseeing. If Reg is busy, other local guides take his guests fishing and sometimes stay at the lodge for dinner. New arrivals are brought up to date on what's biting and where. All in all, it's generally a jovial group with Reg, raconteur par excellence, presiding.

The affable host doesn't need much coaxing to tell lively anecdotes from his unusual past. He was born in the West Indies of English parents and, at the age of twelve, was sent to Britain to be educated. He became an officer in the Royal Air Force and traveled the world until he left to work as a bush pilot in Africa. He later returned to the West Indies, where he ran yacht charters and taught flying. He also taught flying when he first came to New Zealand in 1972, until the first stage of Solitaire Lodge opened four years later.

There are now six large bedrooms, each with open-beam ceilings, a private wood deck, and a fabulous lake view. The spacious penthouse suite, with its 180-degree vista and large spa bath, is popular with honeymooners. In addition to the dining room, two living rooms, both with fireplaces, are available to guests.

The lodge attracts not only top U.S. executives but also senators, film stars, and professional athletes who like to fish and enjoy Reg's entertaining company.

Trout fishing and Reg Turner. That's what Solitaire is all about.

TE ANA FARM

Ngakuru, R.D. 1
Rotorua, (073) 32-720

■

HOSTS: Heather and Brian Oberer.

LOCATION: Twenty miles south of Rotorua.

CATEGORY: Farm stay.

ACCOMMODATIONS: Three rooms, one with private bath.

RATES: Moderate.

INCLUDED: All meals, wine with dinner.

CREDIT CARDS: None.

Anyone meeting the Oberers for the first time will be struck by Heather's peaches-and-cream appearance, but it doesn't take long to realize that her beauty is much more than skin-deep. She and her husband are two of the most gracious farm-stay hosts on the North Island. When they say, "We hope people will make themselves completely at home," they mean it.

The Oberers collect new arrivals at the airport or bus (coach) station in Rotorua and bring them back to Te Ana, where they welcome them with a cup of coffee or tea and some of Heather's home-baked treats.

The hostess is really happy when people pull a stool into the kitchen and chat with her while she fixes dinner. "We both think hospitality is very important," says this transplanted Australian who came to New Zealand twenty years ago.

The coffee table in the living room of their modern home is laden with books and other remembrances sent by grateful former house guests. "We still correspond with many people," Heather told me, "because we became so fond of them when they stayed with us."

The whole family, which includes three delightful teen-agers, devotes time to the guests. Brian takes the visitors out across the five-hundred-acre farm in a four-wheel-drive vehicle; the children accompany those who wish to ride horses or walk to an adjacent lake for trout fishing or canoeing. Heather joins in for a game of tennis. The Oberers run 150 goats, 130 dairy cows, and 800 sheep, and everyone is invited to help with the milking and feeding. Heather and Brian also take guests to visit their neighbor who raises deer.

Because there is so much to do on the farm and in the area, stays with the Oberers should be for a minimum of two nights. In addition to activities on their property, a boat trip to the Orakei Korako thermal region, waterskiing, golf, and a four-wheel-drive trip in the surrounding back country can easily be arranged for a slight charge. On Sundays guests can attend the little interdenominational church in Ngakuru, and on any day the peaceful rural surroundings are a relaxing respite from the rigors of touring.

The accommodations at Te Ana are as pleasant as the hosts. Two rooms have double beds and one has twins. The bathrooms have recently been redone and now resemble the pictures in fancy home-and-garden magazines. The homestead dates from 1937 but was substantially remodeled in 1978. Throughout the house, family antiques are mixed with attractive contemporary furniture.

Mealtimes are also a mix of casual and traditional. Lunch is a relaxed affair for which Heather serves quiche and salad or homemade pizza, but in the evening she switches to lace and silver and prepares a roast lamb dinner or an imaginative dish like lamb en croute or lamb stir-fry. The dessert is usually pavlova when overseas visitors are in the house. (Pavlova, the national dessert, is a meringue concoction served with fresh fruit.) And, for the benefit of travelers, lamb chops are available for breakfast.

Heather's pavlovas are very pretty, and, like the cook who makes them, it isn't just the appearance that is pleasing.

KOHA LODGE

50 Koha Road
Taupo, (074) 87-647
∎

HOSTS: Pat Gluyas and Lindsay Turner.

LOCATION: Fifty-two miles south of Rotorua.

CATEGORY: Bed and breakfast inn.

ACCOMMODATIONS: Three rooms share two baths.

RATES: Moderate.

INCLUDED: Breakfast.

CREDIT CARDS: None.

RESTRICTIONS: No children.

Depending on the season, Pat Gluyas greets new arrivals at Koha Lodge with either a cold beer or a hot cup of tea or coffee. And regardless of the time of year, fresh flowers and fruit will be waiting in the guest bedrooms. These are only some of the little extras Pat and Lindsay thoughtfully provide.

In addition, they use their car to pick up visitors when they arrive in Taupo and will take people around sightseeing or out for a picnic. They also loan golf clubs when necessary and help guests decide how to spend their time.

Koha Lodge, the large home that Lindsay and Pat share, is located about a mile from the center of Taupo (pop. 13,000) in a modern middle-class neighborhood.

One of the well-appointed guest rooms has a double bed and a beautiful view of Lake Taupo. From the windows of the twin-bedded room, steam can be seen wafting from the Craters of the Moon thermal area. A third room has one single bed. Guests don't share bathrooms with hosts, and Pat kindly leaves coffee- and tea-making supplies on a table in the hallway outside the bedrooms.

Downstairs, visitors are welcome to use the television room or the large, attractive living room, where a grand piano sits in front of a picture window. An enclosed thermal pool is also available, and the hosts supply terry robes for guests who haven't brought their own.

Lindsay is a schoolteacher, but he arrives home in time to help Pat prepare the elaborate four-course dinners that are available for an extra charge of about $13, including wine and cocktails. Although the menu changes frequently, it almost always offers pheasant in one form or another because Pat's son raises them in the South Island. Sometimes she serves pheasant soup; at other times marinated pheasant en casserole with grapes and walnuts might be offered. Venison, chicken, rabbit, and duck are also featured.

Because it is illegal to sell trout in New Zealand, it is never seen on menus in restaurants. However, Pat and Lindsay offer their diners a "complimentary" first course of this popular fish. Another special treat is their homemade kiwi-fruit sorbet.

Three-course lunches are also provided for an additional $7. These meals usually start with soup and feature a fish entrée and a dessert of New Zealand cheeses.

If guests don't eat lunch at Koha Lodge, it's because they're out fishing, horseback riding, hunting, playing golf, or sightseeing.

Lake Taupo is the largest lake in New Zealand (on a map of the country it looks like a big hole in the middle of the North Island) and is renowned for good trout fishing.

During the winter, sportsmen can get quite chilled out on the lake, and hot mulled wine is Pat's method for getting them warm again.

It's ironic that many Americans travel to New Zealand to go fishing, because all the rainbow trout in the country are descended from eggs brought from California in 1884.

This interesting fact is just another little extra thoughtfully provided by the hosts at Koha Lodge.

HUKA LODGE

P.O. Box 95
Taupo, (074) 85-791

■

HOSTS: Monique and Co Engels.

LOCATION: Outside Taupo on the Waikato River.

CATEGORY: Country lodge.

ACCOMMODATIONS: Seventeen rooms, all with private bath.

RATES: Very expensive.

INCLUDED: Breakfast, dinner, and pre-dinner drinks.

CREDIT CARDS: All major.

The "new" Haku Lodge, which opened in 1985, is as cosmopolitan as the visitors it attracts. The owner, Alex van Heeren, a Dutchman, immigrated to New Zealand in 1982. Two years later, the wealthy shipping and steel magnate bought the half-century-old fishing lodge with the intention of renovating it and "making it the finest in the Southern Hemisphere." He soon realized that to reach his goal he would have to raze the existing buildings. All that remains of the original structures are a few restored glass doors, some pewter water goblets, and a cat named Mittens.

Van Heeren brought European ideas to Huka and imported Continental talent to carry them out. Co and Monique Engels, the resident managers, have worked in hotels in England, Hong Kong, Switzerland, Belgium, and their native Holland.

The decor of the property they now oversee is drawn from several national styles. The main building is done in a Scottish sporting-lodge motif. An attractive tartan upholstery in navy, hunter green, and red covers chairs and throw pillows in the Lodge Room where guests gather together for pre-dinner drinks. The pattern is carried out in carpeting that runs from this room into the library and dining room, where European antique furniture and paintings, many depicting hunting scenes, create a conservative ambiance. The tartan is also featured on specially designed china used at the breakfast bar.

The bedrooms are tastefully decorated in shades of beige and gray with touches of olive green and white. The king-size beds and open-beam ceilings are reminiscent of California, whereas the wispy white mosquito netting arranged above headboards seems more African than Kiwi. Heated towel rods and European-style showers carry out the international decor.

If guests arrived at Huka Lodge after dark and could only see the interiors of the buildings, they might have a hard time believing they were in New Zealand. But as soon as dawn broke and the surroundings became visible, there would be no doubt. The Waikato River, rushing and bubbling between its willow-draped banks, is only a stone's throw from bedrooms where French doors open onto individual verandahs. The guest cottages, interspersed among native trees, are connected by stone pathways. An expanse of lawn leads down to the river; Huka Falls are just a few hundred yards away.

Mornings begin with venison and wild boar sausages, made especially for the lodge, or whitebait fritters, trout (if caught and donated), or traditional bacon and eggs. Guests sit together at long black-oak tables and discuss the day's possible activities. Huka is most famous for its fishing, but hunting, horseback riding, golf, tennis, hiking, river rafting, and skiing are also popular. A large hot tub and all-weather tennis courts are on the premises.

Breakfasts are popular, but it's the game and seafood dinners, featuring the best New Zealand has to offer, on which the lodge has built its reputation. The five-course repasts feature main courses of wild boar, venison, roast turkey, pheasant, or lamb, accompanied by garden-fresh vegetables and delicate sauces. An extensive range of imported and domestic wines is available. (Children under sixteen dine separately.)

These gourmet meals would surely please Alan Pye, the man who founded the lodge. Pye camped on the banks of the Waikato River above Huka Falls in 1930 and discovered what he was sure must be one of the best stretches of trout-fishing water in the world. He proceeded to buy the land, clear it, and, with his wife, set up a rudimentary fishing hostel. Guests slept in tents, but Alan's wife, Leila, fed them well. The hospitality of Huka Fishing Lodge, as it was known then, and the thrill of fishing the Waikato became renowned among anglers the world over.

Although the decor of the new Huka Lodge has taken on a cosmopolitan appearance, I think Mr. Pye would be happy to know that the lodge still provides a cuisine, a tranquil setting, and a fishing experience that are unmistakably Kiwi.

PUKAWA FARM

Omori Road, R.D. 1
Turangi; (0746) 5135

■

HOSTS: Jinks and Richard Fox.

LOCATION: Forty miles southwest of Taupo.

CATEGORY: Farm stay.

ACCOMMODATIONS: Three rooms share one bath.

RATES: Moderate.

INCLUDED: All meals, wine with dinner.

CREDIT CARDS: None.

You'd never know from looking at it, but Jinks and Richard only paid a case of whisky for their comfortable white colonial farmhouse. Of course, it cost much more than that to move it from nearby Taumarunui to their land at the south end of Lake Taupo. The house, which was built in 1910, is typical of the single-story "villa" style that was popular at that time.

The man they bought it from wanted the house removed so he could use his property for something else; the Foxes decided that a new abode was just what their 1,100-acre farm needed.

The arrangement seems to have worked out very well. The home is perched on an escarpment 350 feet above the lake, and there is a good view from the garden and verandah. Unfortunately for tennis players who are trying to concentrate, the view from the court is also great — and rather distracting.

Richard and Jinks are a delightful couple and indefatigable travelers. They lived in the Middle East for several years while he was employed by the United Nations as a military observer, and their house is dotted with souvenirs from around the world. A table in the hallway holds a collection of sheep models made of various materials in a variety of sizes and styles. The walls in the "loo" are covered with postcards from exotic places.

Richard is still interested in military issues; he also plays tennis, skis, hikes, and, of course, runs a successful sheep and cattle farm. He and Jinks met when they were passengers on a ship going out to New Zealand from England. She was setting out on a short working holiday; he was on his way home after a vacation abroad. They now have grown children and, because the offspring have departed, spare rooms for house guests. One room has twin beds, and the other two rooms have one single bed each.

Pukawa Farm is well positioned for athletic visitors. The Whakapapa ski area (ski field) on Mount Ruapehu in Tongariro National Park, less than an hour's drive away, usually operates from June to early November; the shore of Lake Taupo is only a ten-minute walk, and there's an eighteen-hole golf course eight miles down the road in Turangi. The nearby Tongariro River provides a good venue for trout fishing and white-water rafting.

There are three major active volcanoes in Tongariro National Park — Ruapehu, Ngauruhoe, and Tongariro — and scenic flights over these sometimes smoking cones are available.

The area around the Foxes' farm is rich in Maori history, and Richard and Jinks often participate in activities on the local marae, or tribal land. When Prince Charles made an official visit to the marae in 1981, Jinks was asked to help prepare the sweets for the banquet he was offered. Because it was *her* version of the national dessert the future king chose to eat, Richard refers to it as "the royal pavlova."

Jinks describes the meals she serves to house guests as "good home cooking," but, having sampled them myself, I'd say that she'd be justified — on two counts — if she referred to them as "princely."

DAWSON FALLS LODGE

Manaia Road, R.D. 29
Kaponga, (0663) 5457

■

HOSTS: Jeni and Noel Quince.

LOCATION: Mount Egmont National Park, forty miles south of New Plymouth.

CATEGORY: Historic hotel.

ACCOMMODATIONS: Nine rooms, all with private bath.

RATES: Moderate.

INCLUDED: Breakfast.

CREDIT CARDS: MasterCard and Visa.

The isolated location of Dawson Falls Lodge has caused more than a few guests to comment that the hotel would make a good setting for an Agatha Christie novel, but to me the lodge feels more cozy than mysterious. Its remote position, one-third of the way up the forested slopes of Mount Egmont, means that privacy and peace exist uninterrupted by television, radio, or newspapers; only a radio telephone links Dawson Falls to the outside world.

"A tree could fall across the road and we'd all be stuck here," explained Jeni, but that didn't seem like much of a threat. I knew that a hydroelectric generator (made in America) would keep the kitchen powered and that between meals I could hike the many trails that wind around the mountain.

Dawson Falls Lodge was built in 1896 by the Egmont National Park Board. It remained a public facility until the early 1970s when a local man purchased it and began transforming it into an Alpine-style mountain lodge. He called on the large Swiss population in the area to help him paint delicate mountain flowers on the furniture and wall paneling he crafted from white pine and Douglas fir. All nine bedrooms now have wooden ceilings, and paintings of Alpine scenes decorate the walls. Thick gingham-covered down comforters cover the beds, and cheerful curtains hang from hand-carved wooden cornices. Each room has its own bathroom, some with huge old tubs with gilded claw feet.

A stroke of luck helped Jeni and Noel Quince, a charming Australian couple, to buy the lodge in 1984. Jeni's mother sent them a package from New Zealand, the contents of which were wrapped in newspaper. Noel took the paper out and read an advertisement that said a Swiss-style Alpine lodge on Mount Egmont was for sale. They phoned right away, sold their home in Brisbane, and moved to Dawson Falls.

In spite of the fact that the present owners aren't from Switzerland, Swiss coffee-basted roast leg of lamb remains the house dinner specialty. Also served are traditional New Zealand roast dinners, casual lunches, and hearty Kiwi bacon-and-egg breakfasts.

In addition to hiking around the mountain, visitors often tour the Pukeiti Rhododendron Trust near New Plymouth. The flowering period at the Trust, which is one of the foremost rhododendron parks in the world, is from September to November.

Many guests come to Dawson Falls Lodge specifically because they want to do nothing. Members of Parliament, New Zealand business executives, and honeymooners savor the privacy and seclusion the lodge affords them. At the same time, a homey atmosphere prevails as people sit around the fire reading or playing Scrabble between nature walks.

Jeni says she "likes to talk with guests, but not get in their way." And she's careful not to "bore honeymooners with chitty-chat."

The Summit Room with its four-poster bed is my favorite. On a recent night in this room, I pulled the quilt up to my chin, listened to rain spattering against the windows, and prayed a tree would fall across the road.

RIVERSIDE INN

2 *Plymouth Street*
Wanganui, (064) 32-529

■

HOSTESS: Sylvia Pover.
LOCATION: Central Wanganui.
CATEGORY: Bed and breakfast inn.
ACCOMMODATIONS: Thirteen rooms, one with private bath.
RATES: Inexpensive.
INCLUDED: Breakfast.
CREDIT CARDS: American Express, MasterCard, and Visa.

The Riverside Inn is an archetypical Kiwi B & B. The two-story white Victorian is surrounded by lawn and a colorful border of flowers. Inside, the bedrooms have high ceilings and are furnished with antique dressers and armoires and lots of healthy, green house plants. Four of the spacious rooms have French doors that open onto a verandah.

Sylvia Pover, the inn's hostess, owned a small bed and breakfast in Cornwall before immigrating to New Zealand in 1974, so she's had plenty of experience in making people feel welcome.

"I like to think that when my guests leave they feel they've left a friend," Sylvia told me.

Her helpful attitude reflects these sentiments. She drives to the airport or bus station to collect new arrivals, takes people sightseeing if they don't have a car, and is always available for a friendly chat. In addition, she does guests' laundry and keeps fresh flowers in the bedrooms. At breakfast everyone is introduced to each other, and Sylvia polls them to see if there's a video movie she can rent for them to watch together in the evening.

It was Sylvia who first told me about John Hammond and his rural mail deliveries. If it wasn't for her, I wouldn't have known that for only $8 visitors can ride along with congenial John as he brings mail, groceries, and sundry items to isolated country homes.

Holly Lodge Estate, where there is a winery, a pottery shop, and a craft room where local women create old-fashioned porcelain dolls, is another enjoyable Wanganui activity. Sylvia will drive guests to Holly Lodge, but for those who have the time,

Riverside Inn

it's fun to take the paddle steamer up the Wanganui River.

The inn, which is right across the street from the river, was built as a private country residence in 1895. It later became a nursing home and in 1927 was converted into the Braemar Private Hospital. During this period, a wing was added, which explains why the present bedroom doors are unusually wide — they were built to accommodate hospital beds.

The operating room is now a laundry room, and the dumbwaiter is no longer used for transporting patients, but Sylvia suspects there is one holdover fom the inn's previous life — she calls him "Jack." It's him she blames for turning pictures askew and for moving the gauge on the toaster, causing bread to burn. She says he's a mischievous but friendly ghost who makes his presence known only when he gets lonely.

The Riverside Inn, which became a B & B in 1979, is equally popular with overseas visitors and New Zealanders. When I last stayed there, several rooms were occupied by members of a team of senior men who were in town to compete in a croquet tournament. During the same visit, I met New Yorkers and Chicagoans at breakfast and shared with them the delicious raspberries I had picked at Windemere Gardens the previous day.

Most guests have dinner across the street at the Riverina Restaurant, which specializes in seafood and steaks, but others prefer Bassano's in the Bryvern Motor Inn, where traditional

Italian food is served.

A Continental breakfast is included in the tariff at the Riverside Inn, and a cooked meal is available for an extra $2. Either way, cereal, juice, tea, coffee, and toast are offered. If the latter item appears charred, remember, it's Jack who's to blame, not Sylvia.

MAUNGARAUPI COUNTRY ESTATE

Leedstown Road, R.D. 1
Marton, (0652) 6735
■

HOST: James Anson.
LOCATION: Forty miles northwest of Palmerston North.
CATEGORY: Country lodge.
ACCOMMODATIONS: Two rooms, each with private bath.
RATES: Expensive.
INCLUDED: All meals, cocktails, wine with dinner,
and sightseeing.
CREDIT CARDS: All major.

It isn't only in England that financial survival has deemed it necessary for historic family estates to be opened to the public. Similar problems exist in New Zealand for those who are trying to maintain a mansion. James Anson's Maungaraupi Country Estate, which has been referred to as "a Kiwi Woburn Abbey," is a good example.

The nine-thousand-square-foot English Tudor residence was built by Jim's grandfather, William Swainson Marshall, in 1906 and has remained in the family ever since. To care for it properly, Jim has recently begun taking visitors on a paying-guest basis.

The home is a veritable storehouse of New Zealand pioneer history and family memorabilia. In the library a leather folder contains copies of letters Jim's great-grandmother sent back to friends in England between 1843 and 1853. Above the stairway an elaborate gilded frame holds a portrait of William Swainson, Jim's great-great-grandfather. The wooden door frame of the billiard room is notched to show the heights of various generations of growing occupants, starting with "Mary — 4/1/09" and continuing through Jim's four children.

The structure of the house is also of interest. Its twenty-one rooms have twelve-foot ceilings, leaded windows, and beautiful rimu woodwork. In addition to the billiard room and the library, the downstairs consists of a huge dining room, a grand entrance hall, and a large parlor. Except for the library, each of these rooms has a working fireplace, which Jim keeps stoked in chilly weather. Upstairs, two of the eight bedrooms are set aside for guests. Both are spacious and comfortable.

The mansion is set in the midst of the hundred-acre property with a view of surrounding farmlands and gardens. Jim keeps a few deer, sheep, and cattle, but Maungaraupi is no longer a big working farm. Instead, its owner takes great pride in the gardens that border the house: hydrangeas and roses bloom throughout the summer; magnolias and rhododendrons flower in early spring.

The driveway to the lodge winds for half a mile through native and English trees planted by Jim's grandfather. This woodland area attracts bellbirds, wood pigeons, pheasants, thrushes, white cockatoos, tuis, and fantails, as well as other species of indigenous and imported bird life.

A part of the Maungaraupi's acreage is used for growing asparagus, but because Jim has turned the management of the farm over to his son, he's free to devote himself to house guests. He happily demonstrates sheep shearing or puts his sheep dogs through their paces; he also can arrange fishing expeditions to the upper reaches of the Rangitikei River, where the trout grow up to ten pounds.

For golfers, twelve courses wait within forty minutes of the front door. Because the Rangatira course near Hunterville slopes down quite a bit, a cable car at the end of the eighteenth hole carries players back to the clubhouse. At other area courses the "hazards" are grazing sheep.

Jim is a soft-spoken, gracious host who seems to want nothing more than for people to enjoy themselves at Maungaraupi. The history of his home is important to him, but he is also very aware of his guests' comfort. He employs a cook who prepares tasty traditional farm meals, and he drives visitors through the country-side in his vintage English auto. When I last spoke to him, the host was talking about putting a hot tub in the mansion's bell tower.

This last notion might cause concern among Jim's pioneer ancestors; on the other hand, I'm sure they appreciate all he's doing to preserve the magnificent English Tudor residence they built for the family more than eighty years ago.

EDERDALE

R.D. 54
Kimbolton, (063) 285-728

■

HOSTS: Anne and Graham Wilson.

LOCATION: Thirty-four miles north of Palmerston North.

CATEGORY: Farm stay.

ACCOMMODATIONS: Two rooms share one bath.

RATES: Moderate.

INCLUDED: All meals, wine with dinner.

CREDIT CARDS: None.

Even though Graham and Anne have been hosting visitors for over fifteen years, they still say, "We've never had anyone we didn't like."

At first I wondered how this was possible, but I soon came to realize that a caring attitude and warm hospitality are the basis for their success.

People who arrive in the afternoon are greeted with a cup of coffee or tea and freshly made pikelets. These small, toothsome pancakes are served with homemade jam and good New Zealand butter. The Wilsons listen carefully during this time to find out their visitors' interests, likes, and dislikes. Anne rarely plans menus ahead of time, choosing to play it by ear and tailor meals to guests' preferences. She accommodates allergies as much as possible; she managed to find substitutes for flour for one man.

Daytime activities are also determined by the company. Many want to work off their pikelets by walking to a nearby river; others request to visit a deer or goat farm, and some people like to take part in the day-to-day activities of the 750-acre sheep and cattle farm. Graham adjusts his schedule accordingly.

The most popular attraction in the area is Cross Hills Gardens and Nursery, where the largest private collection of rhododendrons in New Zealand—over a thousand varieties—are set in eighteen acres of landscaped gardens. Cross Hills is owned by Rodney and Faith Wilson, Graham's brother and his wife, so house guests from Ederdale get preferential treatment. In addition to the colorful rhododendrons that bloom from October to December, deciduous azaleas thrive throughout the parklike grounds.

Cross Hills and Ederdale are both situated a lofty 1,800 feet above sea level and have expansive views of the surrounding hill country. On a clear day it's possible to see Mount Egmont and Mount Rupehu from Anne and Graham's property.

The guest bedrooms, both of which have twin beds, share the panoramic view. One of the rooms has a sink; a bathroom is shared by visitors, but the hosts have their own facilities.

Although the Wilsons hope their company will stay for at least two nights, they do offer a reduced rate for brief overnight stops. Not many people are interested in the lower tariff, however. A woman from Arizona came for a few days and stayed for five weeks. One English couple has been back four times. A pair of Canadians had a two-week visit and are planning to return.

These unusually long periods of time indicate how easy it is to be comfortable around the Wilsons. Their home has a welcoming feel to it, and their kindness causes people to linger.

This sounds like make-believe, but it isn't: As I drove away from Ederdale after my last visit, a beautiful rainbow appeared in the sky, and when I stopped the car to look, I couldn't help noticing that the end of it was hovering over Anne and Graham's house.

CHAYTOR HOUSE

P.O. Box 1130, 18 Chaytor Street
Palmerston North, (063) 86-878

HOSTS: Shirley and Brian Cumings.
LOCATION: Central Palmerston North.
CATEGORY: Bed and breakfast inn.
ACCOMMODATIONS: Nine rooms, three with private bath.
RATES: Inexpensive.
INCLUDED: Breakfast.
CREDIT CARDS: All major.

It's not surprising, considering that Palmerston North is a university town, that many guests at Chaytor House are visiting lecturers or scholars. The B & B is located in a residential neighborhood only a couple of miles from Massey University, and buses run frequently between the two places.

Not long ago, a group of Chinese graduate students stayed at Chaytor House for a period of three months. When they first arrived, their behavior was stiff and formal; Shirley's personality, which is warm and gregarious, must have been a shock to them. However, her friendliness helped them to relax, and by the time they left, they were feeling very much at home. One night they even commandeered the kitchen and prepared a sumptuous Mandarin feast.

Normally, dinners at the inn are more typically Kiwi. Shirley used to serve three courses, but she found that her guests were too full to eat their desserts, so she eliminated the appetizer. Now roast lamb or beef, accompanied by a colorful selection of fresh vegetables, is followed by a generous helping of a homemade sweet. (Dinners cost about $6.)

The Cumingses introduce everyone to each other at mealtimes, and overseas visitors are encouraged to identify their hometown by putting a pin in the world map on the wall of the dining room.

The hosts' amicable attitude is reflected in their inn's decor. Stained-glass windows, lace tablecloths, and a crystal chandelier give a quaint aura to the parlor. Brian's collection of Jim Beam cars and Shirley's silver teapots are on display in the reading room for all to enjoy. Along a big wooden staircase topped with alabaster lamps, three round, frosted windows bear the CH monogram.

The six upstairs bedrooms share one bathroom, but each room has its own sink. Three rooms on the ground floor have private baths, coffee- and tea-making facilities, and separate entrances off a rear patio.

Most Chaytor House guests choose to dine "at home," but a few strike out and try the local restaurants. Da Mario and Medici offer Italian dishes, the Bistro and Patrick's are French provincial, and Manelitos serves Kiwi Mexican fare.

In addition to touring the beautiful campus of Massey University, visitors in Palmerston North (pop. 70,000) can stop at the Rugby Museum, a shrine to New Zealand's national sport, and stroll around the Square, a spacious garden area shaded by trees in the commercial heart of the city.

Either Shirley or Brian is usually available to give advice on sightseeing and answer any questions. If they both go out,

Shirley's mother, Mrs. Good, takes over. This sweet, grand-motherly woman has a special talent for making people welcome.

A sign over the door at Chaytor House says, "We meet, we part, and sometimes we remember." I bet their guests *always* remember the friendly attention they receive at this cozy bed and breakfast inn.

OKIOKINGA GUEST HOUSE

88 *Cole Street*
Masterton, (059) 82-970
■

HOSTESS: Robin Andrew.

LOCATION: Sixty-two miles northeast of Wellington.

CATEGORY: Bed and breakfast inn.

ACCOMMODATIONS: Four rooms, none with private bath.

RATES: Inexpensive.

INCLUDED: Breakfast and pre-dinner sherry.

CREDIT CARDS: MasterCard and Visa.

RESTRICTIONS: No children.

The only rule at the Okiokinga Guest House is "People have to let me know what they want." According to hostess Robin Andrew, who issued this directive, this means "Guests must ask for what they want if they don't see it or if it isn't offered."

Robin backs up her stated hospitality policy with action. Recently, an American requested lamb chops for breakfast — and got them. Another guest saw a sweater her hostess had made and asked for a quick knitting lesson — and got it. I requested pumpkin soup, and it was ready within a few hours.

Robin's willingness to please her house guests and meet their needs is readily apparent: one bathroom and shower have wheelchair access; games, cards, and books are made available on rainy days; tea- and coffee-making facilities are provided. She also grows her own vegetables, which are served at dinner either as soup (zucchini, pumpkin, or tomato) or salad. The price of her three-course meal is about $8.

In addition to soup or salad, a typical dinner at the Okiokinga Guest House might include pork fillet (pronounced "fill-it" by

New Zealanders) with apricot sauce and a dessert of fresh fruit salad or lemon soufflé. Afterward, coffee is served in the parlor.

Until 1984 when Robin bought it, the large single-story white colonial house had been a private home. She proceeded to renovate it, totally modernizing the two bathrooms while preserving the old-world appeal. Beautiful stained-glass windows remain in both the interior and the exterior doors. All of the rooms have high ceilings and are spacious, comfortable, and bright. In addition to the large vegetable garden, camellias, fuchsias, and other summer flowers bloom around the house.

Besides being Okiokinga's Jill-of-all-trades, Robin enjoys knitting and practicing the French she learned from her mother, who was born in Switzerland and came to New Zealand after marrying a Kiwi in World War I. The hostess, a former physical education teacher, also keeps herself apprised of area activities so she can pass the information along to visitors.

The National Wildlife Centre at Mount Bruce, seventeen miles north of Masterton, is the region's best known feature. It contains numerous rare and endangered species of birds and lizards native to New Zealand. More than just an animal park, the Wildlife Centre is part of the nation's conservation strategy and conducts breeding programs within its boundaries.

At the Centre, visitors learn that New Zealand has no native land mammals and that, since they didn't need to take wing to avoid being eaten, several birds evolved as flightless. The most famous of these is the kiwi, a brown, hen-sized creature with a long bill, which has become the symbol of the nation.

Robin doesn't accompany her guests on outings, but she's there with a welcoming "cuppa" at the end of the day.

In the Maori language *okiokinga* means "place of rest and retirement." Robin's personal service and warm hospitality justify the name of her B & B.

The East Coast
of the North Island

Because it is slightly off the beaten path, the east coast of the North Island is often overlooked by overseas visitors. However, the area is popular with savvy Kiwis, who appreciate its mild climate and unusual scenery.

The easternmost extremity of the region, the East Cape, is rimmed by Highway 35, which passes through rural settlements and alongside beautiful, often deserted beaches. The East Cape Road is of particular interest just before Christmas, when flowering pohutukawa trees add flashes of crimson to picturesque seascapes.

At the southern end of the coast road, the town of Gisborne (pop. 32,000) is surrounded by rich farmland. Captain Cook christened the area Poverty Bay when he landed there in 1769, but today the name is an ironic misnomer. Corn, citrus, and especially grapes help form the basis of the region's economic importance.

Napier, Hastings, and Havelock North, the three principal communities in the central Hawke's Bay district, share a pleasant climate and are home to affable citizens. Napier has been developed into a popular tourist center and in many ways resembles a British seaside resort. Hastings is known as "the fruit bowl of New Zealand," but Napier and Havelock North are just as prolific in the production of fruit, vegetables, and wine.

Dannevirke, in southern Hawke's Bay, is the focal point of a prosperous dairy and sheep-farming region.

MAKARIKA STATION

R.D. 1
Ruatoria; Ruatoria 201
■

HOSTS: Lesley and Michael Cotterill.

LOCATION: East Cape, seventy-five miles north of Gisborne.

CATEGORY: Farm stay.

ACCOMMODATIONS: Two rooms share one bath.

RATES: Expensive.

INCLUDED: All meals, wine with dinner.

CREDIT CARDS: All major.

RESTRICTIONS: No children under fifteen.

Lesley's English parents needn't have worried that she'd be "living in a mud hut" in the outback of New Zealand if she married Michael. The Cotterills have farmed on the East Cape for five generations, and the house that Lesley was destined to live in is often cited in anthologies as an excellent example of a well-maintained colonial homestead.

However, it's easy to see how more than twenty years ago New Zealand seemed a long way off and a concerned mother and father wondered how their daughter, a product of one of England's best finishing schools, would fare in the antipodes.

The couple met while Michael was traveling in England, and to be able to see him during their long-distance courtship Lesley joined BOAC as a flight attendant.

She couldn't have realized it at the time, but her schooling at Winkfield Place, in Windsor, provided her with just the skills she needs to be a farm-stay hostess.

Surely her alma mater would be proud of the delicious picnic lunches she packs in wicker hampers. Homemade pâté or terrine is accompanied by cold chicken or lobster, when it's in season. A variety of Lesley's chutneys are also included, as are fresh fruit and imported cheeses. Crystal or pewter goblets are tucked in next to a bottle of one of New Zealand's best white wines.

Whereas Lesley is the chef in the household, Michael calls upon his considerable knowledge when selecting the right wine to go with each meal. Many Californians are surprised, as I was, to discover someone living seven thousand miles away who knows so much about new Golden State vintages. Makarika Station may be isolated, but Michael keeps current by reading magazines for wine connoisseurs, just as Lesley devours gourmet periodicals.

Dolly, Lesley's Cessna 180, also helps the Cotterills stay in touch with the outside world. They use the plane to call on friends around the country or to pick up house guests in Rotorua or Auckland. For $125 Lesley can fly three passengers from Rotorua to the Ruatoria airstrip near Makarika. The trip from Auckland costs $250. Lesley is the only woman in New Zealand licensed to pilot this type of plane, and she delights in taking people on air tours. "The price of the flight includes my commentary," she teased.

The station can also be reached by road; Opotiki is three hours in one direction and Gisborne an hour and a half the other way. The hosts will collect visitors who prefer to use commercial airlines at the Gisborne airport.

In addition to superb lunches, Lesley creates wonderful dinners and inviting breakfasts — always relying on local produce. "Quail eggs and smoked salmon are about the only two things we have to buy," commented the hostess as she prepared a whiskeyed hare terrine. (The hare had been annoying Michael by chewing on his kiwi vines.)

Mornings at Makarika begin with early-morning tea thoughtfully served in bed, and continue on to freshly squeezed juice and a choice of hot cakes, fresh and preserved fruit, croissants, or bacon and eggs. The meal is enjoyed in the Cotterills' attractive Danish-modern kitchen.

Dinners, which are more formal affairs, take place in their elegant dining room, where a silver tea service, Oriental rugs, and beautiful antiques create an ambiance not unlike that of an English manor house. "Oh, I wish my mother could hear you say that," said Lesley when I commented on the decor of her home.

I hate to think what Mum would say if she could see her daughter helping out on the three-thousand-acre hill-country station. With 450 cows, 4,200 ewes, and fifteen acres of kiwi fruit there are times when everyone has to pitch in — and finishing school graduates aren't exempted.

TOLAGA INN

P.O. Box 80
Tolaga Bay, Tolaga Bay 856

■

HOST: Ken Leslie.

LOCATION: East Cape, thirty-three miles north of Gisborne.

CATEGORY: Historic hotel.

ACCOMMODATIONS: Eleven rooms, none with private bath.

RATES: Moderate.

INCLUDED: Breakfast and dinner.

CREDIT CARDS: All major.

"The country is agreeable beyond description, and with proper cultivation, might be rendered a kind of second Paradise," wrote an officer sailing with Captain James Cook when the *Endeavour* anchored in Tolaga Bay in 1769. An excellent beach and fertile surroundings inspired these complimentary words and gave the famous explorer reason to retun to the bay in 1777.

I'm not sure what was meant by "proper cultivation," but I suspect that Cook and his mates, who sailed from a land of Tudor pubs, would approve of the Tudor-style Tolaga Inn that is the focal point of the community today.

Because the large hotel, with its leaded windows and coats of arms, looks rather out of place in the rural seaside town, it has been turning heads of passers-by since it was built in the early 1930s.

The Tudor motif is carried out inside, where dark wood paneling and a low, exposed-beam ceiling give the house bar a storybook atmosphere. "In what far country does tomorrow lie?" is carved into the redwood around the fireplace in the bar. The name of the inn's architect, Sholto Smith, is inscribed nearby.

A portrait of Captain Cook hangs in the dining room near a telescope and a limited-edition print of his original map of New Zealand.

Meals at the Tolaga Inn are home-style and satisfying. "No fancy stuff," according to the host, "but very good." A three-course dinner and a hearty Kiwi breakfast are included in the tariff.

The bedrooms are comfortable, but the inn's real draw is the friendly public bar, where nine local darts teams gather on Friday nights. The SRO scene is a great opportunity for visitors who want to savor real country-pub ambiance and rub shoulders with farmers, council employees, and retired people who have relocated to the area. The regular clientele like to tell newcomers about the day a high-spirited patron did not bother to dismount on his way into the bar for a beer—and I suspect the tale gets taller with every retelling.

In addition to darts and pool during pub hours, Tolaga Bay offers a nine-hole golf course, a good swimming beach, and fresh-and salt-water fishing. Captain Cook has not been forgotten: the streets in the town are named after the members of his crew, and a popular walkway leads to Cook's Cove.

The name *Tolaga* was inadvertently chosen for the bay by the explorer, who misunderstood local Maoris who told him either that it was a *"turanga"* (landing place) or that the wind was blowing from the *"teraki"* (northeast). The mistake proved to be significant because Cook was creating the first maps of the area. He labeled the bay "Tolaga" based on what he thought the natives called it. In fact, he had chosen a name most Maoris of the time could not even pronounce.

Though he might be embarrassed at his error, I think Captain Cook would be pleased at the sight of the Tolaga Inn—a touch of old England in the new world he put on the map.

ALOHA TRAVEL LODGE

P.O. Box 2098, 335 Childers Road
Gisborne; (079) 87-525
■

HOSTS: Vera and Ferdy Ferdinando.
LOCATION: Central Gisborne.
CATEGORY: Bed and breakfast inn.
ACCOMMODATIONS: Nine rooms, three with private bath.
RATES: Inexpensive.
INCLUDED: Breakfast.
CREDIT CARDS: None.
RESTRICTIONS: No children under ten.

I'd known Ferdy for several years before I learned he had been a headmaster back in England, but this new information didn't really surprise me. Anyone who had observed the organization and high standards in effect at the Aloha would suspect a pedagogical background.

Breakfast at "Tiffany's," as they call their dining room, is served at "eight o'clock sharp," and guests are greeted with an organized line-up of cereals, juices, fruits, and so on. Ferdy cooks the bacon and eggs to order, and Vera seats everyone as they come in and makes the necessary introductions.

After breakfast, Ferdy dispenses local sightseeing data with the zeal of a professor who cares deeply about his subject. Brochures and maps are provided, as well as precise instructions for getting from one site to the other. Because of his helpfulness and good directions, I was able to drink in the panoramic view from the Kaiti Hill lookout, take note of the statue of Captain Cook at the summit, and find the marker at the water's edge that pinpoints the spot where Cook first landed in New Zealand. I also found the Poho-O-Rawiri meeting house at the base of the hill and took time to appreciate the fine Maori carving and reed work Ferdy had mentioned.

It's only a coincidence that the Aloha, which was built as a private home, was once a dormitory for the local high school. It had already been converted to an inn by the time the Ferdinandos immigrated in 1974.

Vera and Ferdy brought the B & B "up to standard," and they maintain it in immaculate condition. Three ground-floor twin rooms have private facilities, and one of them is suitable for handicapped travelers (a thoughtful alteration made to the eighty-year-old house by its present owners.) The six upstairs rooms have sinks and share two bathrooms. All of the accommodations are equipped with good reading lights, colorful chenille bedspreads, and electric blankets. Tea- and coffee-making facilities are available in the hallway and off-street parking is provided. In the evenings most house guests congregate in the parlor, where the Ferdinandos watch television and play cards or Scrabble with their visitors.

The Aloha is located in a quiet neighborhood three blocks from the center of Gisborne. Several restaurants are within walking distance, and one, L'Escalier, is practically next door. The decor of this spot isn't particularly interesting, but the food (steak, chicken, fish) is good. Those who wish to go farther afield can consult the file of menus the Ferdinandos keep handy. The Arnhem, at the marina, serves a mixture of French and Kiwi fare; Bread and Roses, a BYO on the corner of Lowe Street and Reads Quay, offers interesting dishes such as ratatouille, chilled apple or banana soup, and various kinds of quiche.

Ferdy and Vera don't prepare dinners at the Aloha, but unless it's very late, they're on hand for a chat when diners return to the inn. If they've retired for the night, guests can check the clever "in"/"out" board Ferdy made and, if they're the last ones in, turn out the porch light.

Who else but a former headmaster would have devised such an ingenious system?

REPONGAERE

P.O. Box 116
Patutahi, Gisborne, (079) 27-717
■

HOSTS: Midge and Michael Dods.
LOCATION: Twelve miles west of Gisborne.
CATEGORY: Farm stay.
ACCOMMODATIONS: Three rooms, one with private bath.
RATES: Moderately expensive.
INCLUDED: All meals, wine with dinner.
CREDIT CARDS: All major.

There are many flattering comments in Midge and Michael's guest book, but the one that I feel best sums up their property refers to Repongaere as "an oasis of loveliness."

I can't think of a better way to describe their beautiful two-story white colonial homestead, which stands on a hill at the end of a long winding drive, surrounded by old English trees and colorful flower gardens.

The house was built in 1918 and features polished rimu paneling throughout the interior. A magnificent staircase leads upstairs, where one spacious guest bedroom has a queen bed, a secluded verandah, and a private bath. The other two rooms, both with twin beds, share a bathroom between them. One of the twins is also large and has its own verandah.

Downstairs, a mounted deer head complete with antlers is the focal point of the huge entrance hall. Like the rest of the home, the big farm kitchen and lovely drawing room have fourteen-foot ceilings. The tasteful decor includes a grand piano and many English mahogany antiques.

The house seemed enormous to me, so I was surprised to learn that when Michael's father took over the property in 1940, he felt that the homestead was too big and had fourteen rooms removed.

In addition to the colonial mansion, Repongaere consists of three hundred acres of farmland, most of which is devoted to crops. The Dodses grow corn, cauliflower, citrus, grapes, green beans, barley, and popcorn. Midge manages to incorporate much of this fesh produce into her menus.

A typical lunch consists of homemade soup and quiche with a big salad, followed by fruit. (When the hosts traveled in the United States, they noted Americans' penchant for salads and coffee, so they serve both frequently.)

The five-course dinners at Repongaere feature wild game, with duck, venison, and pheasant being popular main courses. Midge also serves fish, or perhaps lamb stuffed with apricots. Naturally, these dishes are accompanied by a selection of their vegetables.

Besides growing crops, Michael also runs five hundred sheep on their land, and guests are welcome to join in on farm activities. When I asked Midge what her company seemed to enjoy doing most, she replied, "breathing our fresh air." They also like relaxing by the pool, horseback riding, and walking across lush pastures to a lake on the property. Both hosts play tennis on the grass court near the pool, and Midge enjoys playing golf with visitors.

Two good wineries and a swimming beach are only ten minutes away, and a historic Maori meeting house is nearby, too. The Dodses do local sightseeing with guests and collect new arrivals at the airport, coach station, or train station in Gisborne; sailing, hunting, and fishing excursions can be arranged at an extra charge. Because of the number of diversions available, Midge and Michael are happiest when company can stay for at least two nights.

"We treat them as friends and include them in whatever we're doing," said Midge, referring to their house guests. For Michael's part, this includes spinning yarns, or "elaborating on the truth," as he put it.

Come to think of it, I wonder if his father really did take fourteen rooms off the house.

PINEHAVEN HOTEL

42 Marine Parade
Napier, (070) 55-575

■

HOSTS: Eve and Bill Dennis.
LOCATION: Hawke's Bay, central Napier.
CATEGORY: Bed and breakfast inn.
ACCOMMODATIONS: Eight rooms, none with private bath.
RATES: Inexpensive.
INCLUDED: Breakfast.
CREDIT CARDS: All major.

Of all the B & Bs in New Zealand, none has a view quite like that of the Pinehaven Hotel, which overlooks Napier's picturesque Marine Parade. The scene is especially appealing at Christmas time, when the Norfolk pines that line the promenade are covered with thousands of tiny white lights.

The inn's front-facing rooms have large picture windows, which provide a good view of the surf and beach activities. The waves are small, but the smell of the sea air is rejuvenating.

The accommodations, most of which are on the second floor, are spacious and cheerful. Dark-green-painted furniture is complemented by pale green wallpaper and attractive bedspreads. Each of the rooms is named after a tree: Oak, Blue Gum, Maple, Tawa, and so on. Redwood has two big easy chairs facing the water, a twin bed and a double. Two showers and one bath are shared by guests.

Like many proprietors of Kiwi B & Bs, Eve and Bill Dennis are English expatriates. In spite of the fact that they've been in New Zealand for many years, they continue to treat their guests to a full British breakfast. The meal begins with cold cereals and porridge, which are followed by bacon and eggs, fried potatoes, baked beans, and sausages. The tables are set with place cards bearing the guests' names.

Tea and cookies brought into the lounge at nine o'clock every evening are another thoughtful touch. The Dennises pride themselves on their hospitality and make every effort to be helpful.

In addition to running the inn, Bill operates Bay Tours, a small company that conducts minibus tours of the Hawke's Bay region.

On one excursion visitors are shown through a factory where sheepskins are processed and the final products are available for purchase. This same trip also stops at a pottery, and later a ploughman's lunch is served in a winery. Bill's most popular tour, "Tread the Wine Trail," calls in at five or six wineries, and ample time is allowed for tasting some of New Zealand's premium vintages.

There are also several attractions within a short walk of the Pinehaven. At the Nocturnal Wildlife Centre, kiwis, moreporks, barn owls, and night herons inhabit a large display area. The aquarium, where Davey Crocodile is the official greeter, is nearby, too.

Eve and Bill don't serve meals other than breakfast, but several dining spots are dotted along the Marine Parade. The Cottage Cafe is good for lunch and teas; Chatters and Castaways are both BYOs. Pickwick's is a quiet French restaurant set in an old house. My favorite place for lunch, Mabel's, is a few blocks away from the water on Hastings Street. At this congenial self-serve cafe, homemade soups, casseroles, quiche, and delicious baked items are offered at very reasonable prices.

Back on the Marine Parade, a row of restored Victorians house some interesting shops. One of these, Vertu, specializes in beautiful hand-blown glass pieces, watercolor and oil paintings, and pottery.

Napier is often referred to as "the antipodean equivalent of a British seaside resort," and the style of buildings along the promenade and the English hospitality at the Pinehaven B & B certainly support that description.

THIRTEEN SIMLA TERRACE

13 Simla Terrace
Napier, (070) 54-475

■

HOSTESS: Ann Robertson.

LOCATION: Hawke's Bay, suburban Napier.

CATEGORY: Home stay.

ACCOMMODATIONS: Two rooms share one bath.

RATES: Moderate.

INCLUDED: All meals, wine with dinner.

CREDIT CARDS: None.

Like many New Zealanders who do home hosting, Ann Robertson provided hospitality for numerous people before she began having guests on a paying basis. Because she's involved in the international service groups Friendship Force and Zonta, Ann has frequently provided accommodations for members of these groups.

As a result, her home is dotted with ethnic artifacts visitors have brought to her. A shelf near the front door holds a collection of Japanese figurines, and American Indian pottery from New Mexico is displayed on a table in the living room.

Ann's house, which was built by a former mayor of Napier about twenty years ago, sits on a knoll known as "Hospital Hill" and commands an expansive view of the city and distant mountain ranges.

The two guest bedrooms, one with a double bed and the other with a single, are both spacious. Visitors share a bathroom, and the hostess has separate facilities.

The heated towel racks in the bathroom were my first clue that Ann might not have been born a Kiwi. "I've been here since 1965, and I brought part of England with me when I came," she said, referring to the beautiful family antiques and Oriental rugs that help make her living room attractive. A big open fire in this room also gives her house a comfortable, homey feel.

"I left a public relations job in London because I prefer the lifestyle and climate of Hawke's Bay," Ann told me. After arriving in the area, this ambitious lady bought a peach and nectarine orchard, which she ran for twenty years before retiring and moving into town. She's still very interested in horticulture and is a wealth of knowledge on the subject.

Ann enjoys taking guests to visit vineyards and places where fruit is grown, but she also likes to go hiking and to do general sightseeing with her company. She's interested in photography and has discovered the best vantage points for good shots of her area.

The tall stately hostess reminds me of Clare Boothe Luce, so I wasn't surprised to learn that she's interested in politics, as well as classical music — and fishing. She is independent and self-sufficient, but when it comes to her house guests, she does everything she can to see that they get the most out of their stay. She's happiest when travelers write to her ahead of time, so she knows their interests and can organize appropriate activities.

A reduced bed-and-breakfast tariff is available for those who don't want all three meals, but since Ann's a good cook, very few people opt for the lower rate.

No one seems to mind the absence of a television. Recent copies of *Time* and the *Manchester Guardian* are always available, as are a wide variety of books and records.

And with a well-traveled, interesting hostess like Ann Robertson, guests at Thirteen Simla Terrace never lack for good conversation.

SPRINGVALE STATION

Puketapu
Hawke's Bay, (070) 447-589
■

HOSTS: Diane and Roger Alexander.
LOCATION: Hawke's Bay, ten miles west of Napier.
CATEGORY: Farm stay.
ACCOMMODATIONS: Two rooms, each with private bath.
RATES: Moderate.
INCLUDED: All meals, wine with dinner.
CREDIT CARDS: None.

Words like *nice* and *friendly* just don't seem adequate for describing Diane and Roger Alexander. They're the kind of genuine, easy-going people with whom visitors feel comfortable almost immediately. "We treat our guests the way we would treat our friends," Diane told me, and I had every reason to believe her.

The Alexanders' children are as personable as their parents. Geoffrey just started college (university) after spending a year in South Africa as a Rotary exchange student. Another son, Philip, took part in a Rotary exchange in Montpelier, Idaho. Diane and Roger also have a daughter, Wendy. Unfortunately, because all three offspring are away at school, only people who visit during vacation periods (December and January) will get to meet them.

Sagacious travelers will plan their stay at Springvale Station to coincide with the harvesting of their favorite fruit. From November to late February, nectarines, apricots, plums, peaches, and berries are ready. From March to May, grapes, apples, and pears are plentiful and delicious. Diane and Roger don't grow all these things on their farm, but they're readily available from neighboring orchards.

At Springvale, 2,500 sheep, 1,200 cattle, 30 goats, and 2 horses roam over two thousand acres of farm land. Another ten acres are set aside for growing apricots.

The homestead on the large station was built in 1877 and is one of the grandest in Hawke's Bay. The elegant drawing room is decorated in traditional English antiques, original oil paintings, and fine upholstery. The dining room features a kauri table that was made in 1860 and seats ten, plus tall silver candlesticks and an inviting log fire. The billiard room, family room, and kitchen are more casual but still very attractive.

One guest bedroom has twin beds with antique head- and footboards. The occupants of this room have the sole use of the most beautiful bathroom I have ever seen on a farm in New Zealand. Done in teal blue and white, it's just around the corner from the bedroom. The second guest room and bath are detached from the house and located next to the swimming pool.

Diane and Roger often barbecue out by the pool in the summertime and serve dinner on the patio. Of course, the meat, whether lamb or beef, is from their station.

In addition to taking house guests to a deer farm or fruit orchard, Diane joins in for golf or bridge, and Roger takes company around the farm in a Land Rover. Tennis can be played on nearby courts, and trout fishing is also possible.

Both of the Alexanders are avid skiers and travelers, and conversation over pre-dinner drinks and meals often turns to these topics.

Springvale Station is home to two pets: a little white poodle named Snugs and a cat named Puss. Roger jokingly refers to them as "Dogmatic" and "Catastrophe," but in truth, like the humans in this lovely house, they offer a warm welcome to visitors and do everything possible to make guests feel at home.

ARDEN LODGE

P.O. Box 423, Kopanga Road
Havelock North, (070) 777-410
■

HOSTS: Vicki and Rick Lowe.

LOCATION: Hawke's Bay, three miles from Hastings.

CATEGORY: Country lodge.

ACCOMMODATIONS: Five rooms, all with private bath.

RATES: Expensive.

INCLUDED: All meals, pre-dinner cocktails, and wine with dinner.

CREDIT CARDS: All major.

RESTRICTIONS: No children.

After purchasing their art-deco mansion in 1985, Vicki and Rick Lowe took a good look at it and decided that something was missing. "We realized that homes of this style usually had a porte-cochère, a roof projecting over the drive at the entrance to the house, but ours didn't have one," Vicki told me.

"We looked at the original plans and a porte-cochère was included, so we assumed it had fallen off in the 1931 earthquake. In order to have cover for our arriving guests, we decided to build one, and we expected that in the process we'd find the foundations of the first. But no: it became increasingly apparent that we were building the original."

Not only have the Lowes completed Arden Lodge; they've also restored and modernized it without destroying its period appeal.

The off-white house was built in 1926 as a "gentleman's residence" and was later used as a dormitory for a nearby private girls' school. In 1966 it was turned into apartments, and it remained this way until 1985.

Vicki and Rick created five spacious bedrooms, each with private bath, upstairs in the house. The beds have brass head-boards and linens color-coordinated with the draperies. Each room is named after the view it commands and the appellations — *Mahia*, *Kopanga*, *Mt. Erin*, *Te Mata*, and *Waimarama* — are inscribed on brass plates.

Downstairs, classic art-deco windows and doors in the dining room overlook the swimming pool and gardens. "Our dining room table seats eighteen," Vicki said, "but we still manage to create an intimate atmosphere that is conducive to good conversation."

Shortly after Arden Lodge opened in July 1986, the Lowes lured an experienced chef away from the popular Auckland restaurant where he was working. They now serve five-course gourmet dinners nightly. These meals start with soup, perhaps New Zealand green-lipped mussel chowder, and go on to pâté and a first course, which might be salmon mousse or sweetbreads with pernod. The entrée could be veal cordon bleu or pork fillets with sherry almond sauce or fillet of beef with green peppers. The choice of desserts often includes creme caramel, lemon meringue pie, chocolate log, or brandy snaps.

After dinner, guests retire to the drawing room for coffee, port, and homemade chocolates, and then some play billiards on the lodge's full-size antique table. Others choose to pass the evening quietly in the library, which has the feel of a good private English club.

Arden Lodge

Daytime activities include visiting wineries, sightseeing, or playing golf at either of two international-standard courses that are handy to the lodge. The only mainland gannet sanctuary in the world is nearby at Cape Kidnappers. The drive up Te Mata Peak leads to what many feel is the most beautiful scenic lookout in the North Island.

On the seven acres of grounds that surround the Lowes' mansion, guests can play tennis or croquet, stroll through the gardens, or swim. A helicopter pad is available for those who wish to go flightseeing or to be whisked away on hunting or fishing excursions.

Arden Lodge makes a good resting place for the travel-weary. Breakfast can be served in bed, and no one would bat an eye if a house guest did nothing more ambitious than lounge by the pool all day. A chauffeur/guide is on call for those who would like to visit private gardens and historic homes, some of which are normally inaccessible to the public.

The Lowes collect guests at the airport in Napier and drive them back to Arden Lodge, where they enter the house through the "original" 1985 porte-cochère.

HAPUA STATION

Private Bag
Havelock North, (070) 51-623
■

HOSTS: Dinah and Anthony Williams.
LOCATION: Hawke's Bay, nineteen miles from Hastings.
CATEGORY: Farm stay.
ACCOMMODATIONS: Three rooms share one bath.
RATES: Moderate.
INCLUDED: All meals, wine with dinner.
CREDIT CARDS: None.

Family, both younger and older generations, is very important to Anthony and Dinah Williams. Their three children are away at school, but dozens of photos adorn shelves and tables in the living room, and when they speak of their "kids," the love and warmth are obvious.

A still life done by Anthony's mother is also in the living room, and a portrait of ancestor William Williams hangs in the dining room.

Anthony speaks with pride of the New Zealand pioneers from whom he is descended. William Williams and his brother Henry came to the Bay of Islands in the early 1820s as Church of England missionaries. They started a school for Maoris, and, because he had learned their language, Henry was chosen to translate the all-important Treaty of Waitangi for the natives.

When the Williams family held a reunion in Paihia in 1973, eight hundred people attended.

The emphasis on family gives Dinah and Anthony's home an informal, comfortable feel. Children are welcome, and those under the age of twelve are charged half price.

Two of the spacious guest rooms in the single-story colonial have twin beds; the other has a double and a twin. The whole house, including the bedrooms, is warm even in the middle of winter.

In spite of the fact that they've been doing farm stays since 1977, the hosts seem genuinely interested in their house guests. If the weather is good, they take visitors to their beach cottage, which is thirty minutes away, for a picnic and a swim. They will also drive company to the top of Te Mata Peak for the sitting-on-top-of-the-world view of surrounding farmland, mountains, and sea.

Warm summer evenings are spent chatting in the sun room; on cool nights Anthony lights a fire, and the talking, and sometimes bridge playing, takes place in the living room. The Williamses also enjoy walking or driving guests over their expansive, hilly property where they run 4,500 sheep and 200 beef cattle and grow pine trees.

Dinah serves delicious meals based on fresh farm produce. Rolled stuffed lamb loin, with salad and lots of fresh vegetables, is the specialty of the house. Because many of the more than three hundred visitors who have stayed at Hapua Station have been Americans, Dinah thoughtfully offers ice water, big salads, and lots of fresh fruit. Breakfast and lunch are casual affairs that often take place on the patio near the swimming pool and hot tub.

Many house guests consider the Williamses' home a haven in which to relax, do laundry, write postcards, and generally catch up. Others use it as a base from which to explore Hawke's Bay, go on an overland safari to the gannet colony at Cape Kidnappers (October to April), tour wineries, and try their hand at trout fishing.

"We tailor ourselves to our guests," Dinah told me. "We absent ourselves if we sense they want to be on their own, and we have a high level of interaction if we feel they want company."

Because the Williamses place a high value on family, friendship, and community service, they are sincere when they say, "Our visitors come as strangers, but we hope they'll leave as friends."

GURTEENAHILLA

Rua Roa, R.D. 8
Dannevirke, (0653) 45-742
■

HOSTESS: Ann Hardie.

LOCATION: Southern Hawke's Bay, thirty miles northeast of Palmerston North.

CATEGORY: Farm stay.

ACCOMMODATIONS: Two rooms, each with private bath.

RATES: Moderate.

INCLUDED: All meals, wine with dinner.

CREDIT CARDS: None.

The immigrant who built Ann Hardie's house in 1912 must have been feeling a little nostalgic, because he named the residence after his home town in Ireland and had *Gurteenahilla* written out in stained glass above the entrance. This impressive window is just one of the many colorful ones found in the interior and exterior doors throughout the single-story homestead.

In 1918 Ann's family bought the big house, with its lovely stained-glass windows, as well as the four hundred acres of rolling farmland that surrounds it. Wall paneling of native timbers and inherited antiques contribute to Gurteenahilla's homey atmosphere.

Ann and her late husband, John, began home hosting in 1972 as part of the People to People program started by former president Eisenhower. They enjoyed the American farmers who stayed with them and decided they would begin taking guests on a paying basis. "We had also traveled a lot and wished we could stay with families and see how people lived," explained Ann.

Visitors are welcome to join their hostess when she attends the nearby Anglican (Episcopalian) church, her flower-arranging club ("floral art group"), or the local chapter of the Country Women's Institute.

House guests can also picnic at a river a short distance from the house, walk trails in surrounding native woodland, tour limestone caves, relax in the garden, or play tennis on the grass court. Ann will take those who don't have a car to see hill-country farming at her sister's, which is about forty-five minutes away.

Gurteenahilla is four miles from the town of Dannevirke (pop. 5,600), which was settled by Danes in 1872. Unfortunately, there is little to remind visitors of its origins as a Scandinavian settlement. However, at Norsewood, thirteen miles north on Highway 2, the Nordic atmosphere is still evident and the Pioneer Museum houses a collection of articles used by the Scandinavian ("Scandy") settlers. At the Norsewear factory, ski sweaters and other woolen clothing can be purchased at less-than-retail prices.

Ann works two days a week as a nurse, but she still has time to prepare tasty home-cooked meals. A typical dinner might be roast beef and up to seven vegetables from her garden. Sometimes she makes soup from mushrooms that grow in the pastures (paddocks), and she's always open to suggestions if anyone has a special request.

Since her four children are grown and no longer living at home, there are two spare bedrooms for company. Both rooms have twin beds; one has an attached bath, and the other has exclusive use of a large bathroom with spa tub just down the hall.

New arrivals will know they've found the Hardie home if they are greeted by a friendly King Charles spaniel who answers to the name Charlie Girl and by a charming hostess whose fair coloring is evidence of her Danish ancestry.

Anyone who is still in doubt can look at the entrance and see if the word *Gurteenahilla* gleams in colored glass above the front door.

Wellington
and Vicinity

San Franciscans visiting Wellington are sure to experience a spell of déjà vu when they see "cable cars reaching halfway to the stars," rows of restored Victorians, and a plethora of Chinese restaurants.

At the same time, Chicagoans will have the best background for dealing with the weather in the city known as "Windy Wellington."

The capital of New Zealand is a cosmopolitan community of foreign-government delegations, business travelers, and politicians. Accommodations are always hard to find, but opportunities for interesting dining and shopping abound.

The best sightseeing attraction is Parliament, which visitors can observe when it's in session. The Beehive, aptly named for its shape, is part of Parliament House and is Wellington's most familiar landmark.

The city is built on a series of hills overlooking a beautiful harbor used by pleasure boats, cargo ships, and the Cook Strait ferries, which carry passengers between New Zealand's two major islands.

The commercial center of Wellington (pop. 320,000) is as busy as its port. Statuesque office towers, the result of the scarcity of land within the constricted perimeters of the city, dominate the thoroughfares. Because of the high earthquake risk, many older buildings have been razed, and Wellington now has the most modern skyline of any urban district in New Zealand.

Day's Bay is a pleasant suburb, and the remote setting of Palliser Bay offers a complete respite from city life.

AMBASSADOR TRAVEL LODGE

287 *The Terrace*
Wellington, (04) 845-697
■

HOST: Phil Smees.
LOCATION: Central Wellington.
CATEGORY: Bed and breakfast inn.
ACCOMMODATIONS: Thirty-six rooms, ten with, private bath.
RATES: Moderate.
INCLUDED: Breakfast.
CREDIT CARDS: All major.

Phil Smees prides himself on the hearty three-course dinners he serves his guests. "I cook them myself and I don't get many complaints," says the host.

The meals start with a homemade soup, which is followed by a roast, steak, or chops and several colorful vegetables. Dessert and coffee are also included for the $8 charge. The meals are by no means gourmet, but on a rainy Wellington night most people are delighted to be able to eat in the Ambassador's pleasant dining room rather than trudge through the storm in search of dinner.

Lunch is not available at this B & B, but a satisfying, stick-to-the-ribs Kiwi breakfast is included in the tariff.

The meals and the convenient central location on the Terrace near Ghuznee Street contribute to the Ambassador's popularity with overseas budget travelers. The availability of off-street parking is another big plus. Even though the rambling eighty-year-old house contains thirty-six bedrooms, it's quite common to see a No Vacancy sign in the window.

Ten of the rooms have private baths (showers, no tubs) and color televisions. The other rooms have sinks and share an abundance of showers and toilets dispersed throughout the building. The furnishings are best described as serviceable, but every room is maintained in a clean and tidy condition.

The Ambassador lacks central heating, but each room has its own small unit, and the beds are equipped with electric blankets. Coffee- and tea-making facilities are provided in the hallway on the second floor. There are two guest parlors, one with television and one Phil refers to as a "conversation lounge." It's not at all uncommon for visitors to meet at breakfast or in one of the lounges and then team up for the next day's sightseeing.

It's only a short walk to the Wellington Public Relations Office on the corner of Mercer and Victoria Streets, where information on the city's attractions can be found seven days a week. In addition, sightseeing tours depart twice daily from the New Zealand Tourist and Publicity Travel Office on Mercer Street. These escorted bus trips take in the Parliament buildings, Old St. Paul's Church, the Lady Norwood Rose Garden, cable cars, and the scenic drive up Mount Victoria.

Several good dining spots are within walking distance of the Ambassador. I like Mahoney's in the Gresham Plaza Arcade on Lambton Quay for lunch or tea. Their specialty is a hot beef sandwich, but they also serve good salads, pâté, and quiche, and they make wonderful cappuccino.

Suzy's on Willis Street is open seven days a week until nine o'clock and is thus a rare find in Wellington. At this self-serve BYO, sandwiches, salads, steaks, and various hot meals are available.

However, it's hard to beat Phil Smees' home cooking — especially on a wet and windy Wellington evening.

BALCAIRN PRIVATE HOTEL

151 Ghuznee Street
Wellington; (04) 842-274

■

HOSTS: Kathryn and Kevin Wilson.

LOCATION: Central Wellington.

CATEGORY: Bed and breakfast inn.

ACCOMMODATIONS: Nine rooms, none with private bath.

RATES: Inexpensive.

INCLUDED: Room only.

CREDIT CARDS: MasterCard and Visa.

American visitors may have the nagging feeling they've met Kevin Wilson before — and, in a way, they have. As an actor, he's been featured on U.S. television in advertisements promoting New Zealand lamb.

When he isn't on stage or in front of the camera, Kevin and his wife, Kathryn, run the Balcairn, a cute B & B in central Wellington.

"Even guests who don't recognize him as an actor take notice of him," Kathryn told me, "because he does much of the housework and that surprises people."

Kevin's "housework" involves looking after the nine guest bedrooms in their seventy-year-old house, which is actually two identical homes that were joined when the wall between them was removed in 1959.

Each of the cozy rooms is decorated in a different way, giving them the sense of being spare rooms in a big family home. The potpourri of furnishings, including a few antiques, has character. "It's just whatever we've been able to pick up," Kathryn explained.

The American prints in some bedrooms were acquired at auction from departing United States embassy staff members. The Wilsons also display their collection of original New Zealand paintings in the hallways.

There is no pretense at being other than what they are. As it says on their brochure, "The Balcairn is a budget hotel with limited facilities. We cater for the busy traveller who wants to keep accommodation costs down."

What the brochure doesn't say is that Kathryn and Kevin are a friendly young couple who go out of their way to be helpful.

They're on hand night and day to answer questions and give advice. Kevin is in a particularly good position to recommend various local theatrical events. Wellington has two excellent venues for live productions: the Downstage Theatre and the Circa Theatre.

When it comes to dining, the Wilsons agree that for pub food the 1860 Victualling Company can't be beat. This self-serve carvery, which is open Monday to Saturday, is located in the AMP Building on Lambton Quay. Roast meals (beef, pork, or lamb) are the specialty, but steaks and seafood are also available.

One of my favorite spots in Wellington is the Pâté Shop on Oriental Parade, where, in addition to all kinds of pâté, they serve soup, salads, cakes, and other things.

Breakfast isn't included in the tariff at the Balcairn, but it's available for an extra charge ($1 for "just toast"; $2.50 for bacon and eggs).

"We do not supply an evening meal," states the Balcairn's brochure, "because we do not have a separate dining room. There are many restaurants within easy walking distance of the hotel, ranging from simple takeaways to expensive nosh houses and trendy cafes. However, for those who find they cannot go out for their evening meal we can offer some comfort in the guise of a packaged TV dinner."

This kind of honesty isn't usually the stuff of hotel brochures, but it must make friends. The majority of Kathryn and Kevin's guests are repeat visitors.

TINAKORI LODGE

182 *Tinakori Road*
Thorndon, Wellington, (04) 733-478 *or* (04) 729-697
■

HOSTS: Gloria and Jack Hastings.
LOCATION: Central Wellington.
CATEGORY: Bed and breakfast inn.
ACCOMMODATIONS: Eight rooms, none with private bath.
RATES: Inexpensive.
INCLUDED: Breakfast.
CREDIT CARDS: All major.

Gloria Hastings has lived in New Zealand for fifteen years, but she hasn't forgotten that her fellow Americans love peanut butter, so she makes it available at breakfast. She also serves her compatriots hot toast, another rarity since Kiwis prefer theirs cold.

These treats are part of the Continental breakfast included in the tariff at Tinakori Lodge. The meal is served in a pretty little dining room, where guests are seated at round tables covered with pink cloths. During the winter, an open fire takes the chill off the morning air.

Gloria and her Kiwi husband, Jack, opened their attractive bed and breakfast inn in June 1986 and have been busy ever since. Eight bedrooms, each with its own television and sink, are located on the ground floor of a restored two-story Edwardian house that is more than 120 years old. The building is cream-colored with striking green and burgundy trim, and the spacious rooms are tastefully decorated with bright wallpapers and colorful bedspreads. Three bathrooms are shared between the guests.

The hosts go out of their way to please. A plate of cookies and mints is placed in each room for new arrivals; everyone gets a complimentary morning newspaper; coffee and tea facilities are in the hall; sightseeing information is available. Gloria even baby-sits little visitors when parents want an evening on their own.

Dinner isn't served at Tinakori Lodge, but packaged frozen main courses, to which Gloria adds hot soup, rolls, butter, and dessert, can be purchased for $6.

Those who prefer a more elaborate meal have a choice of several nearby spots, or they can take the fifteen-minute walk or the three-dollar taxi ride to the city center. In addition, the metropolitan bus stops only two blocks away.

Visitors who wish to observe New Zealand's elected officials in action need only walk five minutes to the Beehive and the adjacent large marble building where Parliament meets. The Kiwi government is modeled on the British system, and the Members of Parliament display the same raucous behavior associated with Westminster.

There are two main political parties in New Zealand. The Labour Party is much like the Democrats in the U.S., and the National Party parallels the Republicans. New Zealand is an independent member of the Commonwealth, and Queen Elizabeth II is the official head of state.

Another enjoyable excursion is to the Botanic Gardens via the cable car from Lambton Quay. The Lady Norwood Rose Garden contains 1,850 roses, and 5,000 flowering plants are on display in the Begonia House.

The cable car is reminiscent of San Francisco and can almost be guaranteed to cause a brief spell of nostalgia in people who are familiar with that city by the bay — even in long-time expatriates like Gloria Hastings.

GLEN FERNY

24 Moana Road, Day's Bay
Eastbourne Wellington, (04) 627-202
■

HOSTS: Dorothy Archibald and Bill Walker.

LOCATION: Suburban Wellington.

CATEGORY: Home stay.

ACCOMMODATIONS: Two rooms, none with private bath.

RATES: Moderately expensive.

INCLUDED: All meals, wine with dinner.

CREDIT CARDS: None.

I arrived on the doorstep of 24 Moana Road on a rainy, cold Wellington morning and my mood was as foul as the weather. Besides having wet feet, I was burdened with a horrible headache. In spite of the fact that it was our first-ever meeting, Dorothy and

Bill quickly saw through the mask of pleasantness I tried to wear. While he went to get some aspirin, she heated a bowl of homemade pumpkin soup. I was better in no time.

Most visitors will arrive at Glen Ferny under more sanguine circumstances, but they will still be treated with the care and concern I received.

"Hospitality is very important to us," Dorothy explained. "We enjoy making guests feel welcome."

"And she's got a soft spot for Americans," Bill added.

This "soft spot," I learned, is due to the fact that the hostess's mother was an American and that Dorothy graduated from Mount Holyoke College in Massachusetts.

Her Kiwi father and Yankee mother were married in 1929, and telltale signs around the large house are evidence that its design was influenced by a non–New Zealander. The free-flowing openness of the rooms, the abundance of electrical outlets, and the fact that there are screens (fly wires) on the windows are just three examples.

Dorothy's family has lived on this land since 1904, first in a tent, then in a bungalow, and finally, since 1941, in the house. Her father's family came out from Scotland, and, since the property was originally covered in ponga ferns, they named the house "Glen Ferny," which means "fern glen" in Scottish.

Her mother decorated the ground floor of the home in beautiful blue-and-white-floral Sanderson wallpaper, which she ordered from England. Later, her parents acquired the carpets that had been used for Queen Elizabeth's coronation and installed them on the living room floor. Also in this room are a wonderful collection of English and French antiques.

Upstairs, both guest bedrooms have an expansive view overlooking the harbor. The center of Wellington is seven miles straight across the water, although Day's Bay is actually fourteen miles by road from the city. One of the attractive bedrooms has twin beds; the other has one single bed.

Some of Dorothy and Bill's house guests may recognize the dishes they serve as being *Sunset* recipes. Dorothy's brother, a San Francisco Bay Area pathologist, sends the magazines to her.

In addition to homemade soup, a cheese soufflé and "interesting" breads are frequently featured at lunch time.

"I'm certainly not a microwave lady," said Dorothy, "and Bill's a marvelous chef."

It's not surprising that very few visitors opt for the reduced bed-and-breakfast tariff offered at Glen Ferny. Those who do miss out on delicious meals and a chance to linger at the table with their fascinating host and hostess.

Dorothy taught Asian geography at Mount Holyoke from 1959 to 1965 and has traveled extensively throughout the world. Bill is a retired business consultant who is presently engaged as an industrial chaplain. Both are active in civic affairs and can arrange meetings with local people (including Victoria University faculty) with whom a house guest shares a particular interest.

"We really enjoy people and will do whatever we can to make them comfortable," Dorothy said.

And, as I know from experience, that includes alleviating a nasty headache.

WHAREKAUHAU LODGE

Western Lake Road, Palliser Bay, R.D. 3
Featherston, (0553) 28-581

■

HOSTS: Annette and Bill Shaw.
LOCATION: Sixteen miles east of Wellington, as the crow flies.
CATEGORY: Country lodge.
ACCOMMODATIONS: Five rooms, four with private bath.
RATES: Very expensive.
INCLUDED: All meals, wine with dinner.
CREDIT CARDS: All major.

When does a farm stay become a country lodge? When Bill and Annette Shaw take over one of New Zealand's largest historic sheep stations and add every possible comfort and imaginable recreational activity.

Wharekauhau (pronounced "Forry-cow-how"), the second-oldest Romney stud in the country, still carries ten thousand sheep and five hundred Hereford cattle, but now, in addition to participating in farm activities, guests can try their hand at surfcasting, floundering, trout fishing, snorkeling, waterskiing, jet boating, canoeing, rafting, trail riding, golf, clay-bird shooting, hiking, hunting, and windsurfing.

Wharekauhau Lodge

The lodge is located on a bluff at the foot of the Rimutaka Mountains overlooking the rugged coastline of Palliser Bay. Lush green farmland surrounds the house, and an expansive view of uninhabited beach is visible from most rooms, including the library and parlor.

Many guests arrive by helicopter, which takes only ten minutes from the Wellington airport. Others prefer the floatplane from Picton. Still others opt for the winding two-hour drive via Featherston, especially if they are touring New Zealand in a chauffeur-driven limousine.

A single room without private bath in the original colonial homestead is usually set aside for drivers. The other four rooms, two in the house and two in the newly built cottage, each have private facilities. All quarters are spacious and tastefully decorated.

Three guest rooms have king beds that can be made into twins, and the fourth has a queen. All are equipped with coffee and tea facilities. The luxurious cottage accommodations feature separate dressing rooms and private sea-view verandahs.

Bill and Annette have managed to successfully combine the charm of country living, the solitude and beauty of their isolated location, and the facilities and gourmet cuisine associated with sophisticated sites. Four-course dinners feature local game (pheasant, venison, quail) and products of the sea (lobster, abalone, salmon, trout). Organically grown vegetables and fresh fruit are served in season. Meals are accompanied by New Zealand wines.

Game is even featured on the breakfast menu, in the form of homemade venison sausages. Lunches are light and usually consist of sandwiches, muffins, or a Devonshire tea.

Most house guests are out exploring or sporting at noon; lunch for them comes in the form of a picnic hamper prepared by Wharekauhau. The lodge also provides tackle, bait, wet suits, boats, and whatever else is needed for activities. Professional guides are available at a charge of $25 an hour.

Hunting guide Joe Houghton takes sportsmen to the Rimutaka Mountains, where red deer, wild boar, mountain goat, and hare await, and he provides instruction, dogs, and firearms.

Bill and Annette also have a four-wheel-drive vehicle, and guests can join safari tours to the Cape Palliser lighthouse, the Cape Turakirae seal colony, or the Lake Wairarapa wetlands. These days tours cost $30 to $50 per person with lunch.

In spite of the number of activities, the Shaws' personal service is still the outstanding feature at Wharekauhau.

We limit our accommodations to eight people," Annette explained, "because our guests are very special to us. Nothing is too much trouble."

Happily, this concern for gracious hospitality wasn't lost when Wharekauhau made the transition from Kiwi farm stay to country sporting lodge.

The Sounds and the West Coast

Many visitors arrive in the South Island on the Cook Strait ferry, which makes frequent crossings between Wellington and Picton. Those who do get a preview of the beautiful Marlborough Sounds during the last part of the trip. The three largest sounds — Queen Charlotte, Pelorus, and Kenepuru — are just part of the extensive labyrinth of waterways that provide limitless possibilities for boating, fishing, swimming, and hiking.

Picton (pop. 3,000) is a busy place just before a ferry leaves and immediately after one arrives. Otherwise, it is a quiet town in a scenic location at the head of Queen Charlotte Sound.

Blenheim (pop. 18,000), which calls itself the "Sunshine Capital" of New Zealand, lies to the south of Picton in the center of a major wine-growing district.

Nelson (pop. 33,000) is another place known for its good climate. Many New Zealanders, attracted by the town's beautiful beach and relaxed way of life, retire here. Many others choose it for vacations.

Motueka, which, like Nelson, is sited on Tasman Bay, is the center of an important fruit-, tobacco-, and hops-growing region.

The West Coast offers a distinct contrast to the benign climate and gentle people encountered in the Nelson – Marlborough Sounds area. From Westport to Haast, the west side of the South Island is characterized by its ruggedness. The sea is stormier, the roads are rougher, and the residents have an untamed Wild West quality about them.

Greymouth and Hokitika, once active gold-mining centers, are now supported by the timber trade. Of the many lakes that dot the surrounding country-side, Lake Brunner is one of the most picturesque.

Whataroa is a wide spot in the road that leads to the West Coast's most popular attractions: the Fox and Franz Josef glaciers.

BELLEVUE GUEST HOUSE

34 Auckland Street
Picton; (057) 36-598
■

HOSTS: Carol and Barry Mills.
LOCATION: Seventeen miles north of Blenheim.
CATEGORY: Bed and breakfast inn.
ACCOMMODATIONS: Six rooms, none with private bath.
RATES: Inexpensive.
INCLUDED: Room only.
CREDIT CARDS: MasterCard and Visa.
RESTRICTIONS: No smoking.

People who have stayed at the Bellevue guest house any time in the last twenty years can look their names up in the B & Bs visitors' book. The same volume that was started in 1967, a year after the inn opened, is still in use today.

"Everyone seems to enjoy rereading their comments," said Carol Mills, one of the Bellevue's proprietors.

The Millses' single-story white weatherboard house was built in 1906 on the site where John McDonald, the first colonist to live in Picton, settled in 1849. A verandah wraps around the front and side of the building, which was constructed to house the town clock and later became a rectory. The clay tiles of the roof were originally used as ballast on a ship that came out to New Zealand from Marseilles.

Carol and Barry bought the central-Picton property after immigrating from London in 1981. Today there are six bedrooms, all with sinks. Two rooms have double beds, two have twin beds, one has three single beds, and the other has a double and two singles. Two showers are shared between the guests.

Large, lace-curtained windows capture the sun in the bedrooms, which are well maintained. All have floral wallpaper, chenille bedspreads, and thick quilts.

Breakfast is available at charges ranging from $1.50 for "the Express" to $3.50 for bacon and eggs. "We would also like to be able to offer cream teas wholesome lunches, and light dinners and have plans to do so in the future," said Carol.

The Millses were attracted to New Zealand by its nuclear-free status and the prospect of living a small-community lifestyle. Barry, who was a social worker in England, lost no time in becoming involved in local activities and soon became Picton's recreation advisor. He also set up the South Island Information Centre on behalf of the Town Council.

This experience makes him a valuable source for visitors wanting to explore the Marlborough Sounds and their environs. Both hosts are avid sailing enthusiasts, and Barry is a fisherman and the captain of the local soccer team. Carol enjoys playing badminton and hiking.

The Sounds can be explored on one of the Friendship Cruises — either the Royal Mail trip, which lasts all day, or a two-hour scenic cruise. Either way, passengers get a sense of the history and beauty that are unique to the area.

Those who prefer to tour by road will find that Queen Charlotte Drive from Picton to Havelock affords many vantage points for viewing the Queen Charlotte and Pelorus sounds. Along the way the coast is dotted with safe beaches for waterskiing, swimming, and picnicking.

In central Picton, the Smith Memorial Museum on the waterfront (foreshore) provides a glimpse into the town's past as a Maori settlement, whaling port, and gateway to the West Coast gold rush.

After a day of sightseeing, everyone at the Bellevue is welcome to fix a cup of coffee or tea and relax in front of the log fire in the parlor. It isn't surprising that visitors feel at home at this B & B.

"We treat guests like a part of the family," said Barry. And the positive comments in their visitors' book indicate that this friendly approach is much appreciated.

MARINELAND PRIVATE HOTEL

28 *Waikawa Road*
Picton, (057) 36-429

HOSTS: Edie and Pat McGlory.
LOCATION: Seventeen miles north of Blenheim.
CATEGORY: Bed and breakfast inn.
ACCOMMODATIONS: Twelve rooms, two with private bath.
RATES: Inexpensive.
INCLUDED: Breakfast.
CREDIT CARDS: All major.

Weight watchers beware! An evening supper of pikelets or scones is standard procedure at the Marineland Private Hotel, and Edie McGlory's goodies are hard to resist, especially when they're warm and fresh from the oven. She serves the pikelets, which are small pancakes, with raspberry jam and thick cream; the scones, either cheese or date, are offered with delicious Kiwi butter. This repast is accompanied by tea and coffee, and no one goes away hungry.

Edie doesn't charge for the supper. It's just a nice treat that she enjoys preparing for her house guests.

Also included in the tariff at this pleasant B & B is a cooked breakfast, which includes fruit, juice, cereal, eggs, bacon, tomatoes, sausage, toast, and tea or coffee. It's definitely not for dieters (slimmers).

Edie and her son Pat bought the Marineland in 1985 and have been providing outstanding hospitality for travelers ever since. They even drive to the ferry landing, bus station, or train depot to pick up new arrivals.

In the evening they join guests in the parlor, where everyone gathers to read the newspaper, watch television, and chat. Like the rest of the house, this room is homey and comfortable. The flowers on the mantle are from the garden, which Edie and Pat tend with the same TLC they bestow on their guests.

In addition to colorful nemesias, roses, and gladiola, the McGlorys have a grapefruit tree, which is heavily laden with fruit in season. Near the tree, an attractive swimming pool is available for guests' use.

The inn wears its eighty-five years well. The bedrooms, although not large, are maintained in good repair, and each has its own coffee and tea facilities. One would never know that the house was built as a doctor's residence and office. It remained a private home until 1963, when the first ferry arrived in Picton.

The hosts offer a reduced rate during the winter months, June to August, because there are fewer tourists at that time of year. (The parlor is kept warm, and all beds have electric blankets.)

In addition to outstanding hospitality, the central location of the inn contributes to its popularity. Several good dining spots are within walking distance. This includes the 5th Bank, a licensed restaurant that specializes in traditional New Zealand fare: mussels, steak, seafood, chicken — often with delicious sauces. As the name implies, the building one housed a bank, but the ambiance has undergone a complete transformation and is today warm and cozy.

The Ship Cove, another convenient eatery, specializes in fresh seafood and steak.

Picton is usually a quiet little town whose activity is tied to the ferry timetable, but it became the focus of attention a couple of

Marineland Private Hotel

years ago when a Russian cruise ship sank in Cook Strait. Many of the crew, divers, and salvage engineers stayed at the Marineland for several weeks while the fate of the Soviet vessel was decided.

I wish I could have seen their faces the first time Edie McGlory entered the parlor bearing a tray laden with freshly baked scones and pikelets. It's surprising that no one defected.

SOUTHERN MARINE HOME STAY

P.O. Box 246
Picton, (057) 36-591
∎

HOSTESS: Millie Pickering.
LOCATION: Marlborough Sounds — at home at anchor.
CATEGORY: Something different.
ACCOMMODATIONS: Vary.
RATES: Moderate.
INCLUDED: Breakfast and use of dinghy.
CREDIT CARDS: All major.

"What could be more romantic than sleeping aboard a sailboat in the Marlborough Sounds?" Millie Pickering asked rhetorically. And I had to admit I couldn't think of anything.

Millie, who manages Southern Marine Charter in Picton, devised this stay-aboard plan in 1985, and it has been operating with success ever since.

Guests arrive in Picton and are shuttled by water taxi or charter launch ($15 per person) to a sailboat (yacht) anchored near Arapawa Island in the Sounds. They live on the boat and have the option of taking the dinghy to a nearby farm for meals.

"It's the only program I know of that combines boating and a farm stay," said Millie. And again I had to admit she was right.

It's necessary to either bring sleeping bags or rent them from Millie. The boats vary in size; some are just right for honeymooners, and others can accommodate a family of six. Breakfast is included in the tariff; lunch and dinner are available for an extra charge.

"Some people prefer to lounge around on the boat during the day and then sleep at the farm, and that's ok with us, too,"

Millie explained.

The farm, called "The Castaways," is owned by Pam and Mike Davies, and they happily accommodate visitors any way they can. Lunch, which costs about $4, might consist of cold meats, pizza, salad, or crackers and cheese. Their three-course dinners ($8) include soup, fresh fish or roast lamb, and several vegetables. After dessert, coffee, tea, and cheeses are offered. The vegetables come from Pam and Mike's large garden, so they're as fresh as the "just caught" fish. Wine isn't served at dinner, but those who wish it may bring their own.

Some people enjoy participating in farm activities; others prefer to go fishing, scuba diving, or hiking through the native bush. Diving gear and Windsurfers can be arranged through Millie.

Since the Davieses' children are away at boarding school, there are three spare bedrooms in the house. Guests have a choice of double, single, or bunk beds. The bathroom is shared with the hosts.

The boats are fairly new and fully equipped. Each one has plenty of galley equipment and a radio; Pam and Mike have a telephone and a television at the farm. They also keep lots of books handy and enjoy playing board games with visitors. Their farm can only be reached by boat, so privacy is never a problem.

To whom does this island idyll most appeal?

"We get heaps of honeymooners and a handful of harried executives," answered Millie.

Given the circumstances, the company motto, "Happiness is a Southern Marine Charter," seems most appropriate.

KOANUI GUEST HOUSE

33 Main Street
Blenheim, (057) 87-487
■

HOSTS: Sheila and Len Wall.
LOCATION: Central Blenheim.
CATEGORY: Bed and breakfast inn.
ACCOMMODATIONS: Ten rooms, none with private bath.
RATES: Inexpensive.
INCLUDED: Breakfast.
CREDIT CARDS: None.

The last time I stopped in at the Koanui Guest House I interrupted Sheila and Len, who were in the middle of painting the parlor. Anyone else would have suggested I come back later, but not these two. They stopped where they were and put the kettle on so we could have a cup of tea.

It had been three years since I'd stayed with them, but Sheila remembered which room I'd had and in which bed I'd slept. Not many hosts would be able to recall these kinds of details about their guests, but the Walls are really special people.

If they find out that someone who's staying with them has never picked a peach or visited a winery, they'll take the person out and remedy the situation. They've even driven visitors around the Sounds, in spite of the fact that sightseeing isn't included in the tariff.

Sheila and Len moved to Blenheim from Invercargill after he retired from his job as a professional firefighter. Like many folks from the cold end of the South Island, they were attracted by Blenheim's sunny climate. Both were born in England, the land where B & Bs abound, and perhaps this influenced their decision to buy the Koanui.

The single-story house was built around the turn of the century as a private home, but it became a guest house after a short time. The Walls have decorated the parlor, where the television and coffee and tea facilities are located, with comfortable, family-style furniture. The bedrooms are bright and cheerful — and always very clean. Each room has its own sink, and three showers are shared between the guests.

The Koanui's central location, three blocks from the middle of Blenheim, certainly adds to its popularity, as does the fact that off-street parking is available.

Sheila and Len will go to the airport or coach station to pick up those who don't have a car, and they're very helpful with sightseeing and dining advice.

Blenheim's top attractions are its wineries and the Riverlands Cob Cottage, a restored mud-walled and shingle-roofed pioneer abode (circa 1859) that has been furnished in period style and preserved as a museum. The house, which was built for one of the district's earliest farmers, is located three miles south of town.

The flower gardens in Pollard Park, near the center of town, are also of interest during the spring and summer.

Two restaurants are within a five-minute walk of the B & B. The Walls recommend the carvery at the Raffles Hotel for dinner. They also like the Top Spot Restaurant, which serves steaks and other grilled meals. Both of these places are licensed.

The Peppertree, on the main highway south of town, is a small French provincial restaurant with an infomal ambiance and a tasty cuisine.

I don't know if a pepper tree grows near the restaurant. Sometimes it's hard to understand how some places got their names. One appellation in Blenheim is easily understood, however. Len and Sheila seem to derive a great deal of pleasure from making guests feel welcome at the Koanui. And in Maori *koanui* means "lots of joy."

LAKE TIMARA ESTATE

R.D. 2
Blenheim, (057) 28-276
■

HOSTS: Mo and Graham Sutton.
LOCATION: Eight miles east of Blenheim.
CATEGORY: Farm stay.
ACCOMMODATIONS: Two rooms, one with private bath.
RATES: Moderately expensive.
INCLUDED: All meals, wine with dinner.
CREDIT CARDS: None.

Lake Timara Estate is an enologist's delight. Within a short drive of the seven-hundred-acre farm, six wineries welcome visitors to taste their products and observe their processes.

Cellier Le Brun makes sparkling wine in the *méthode Champenois* in underground cellars. Te Whare Ra creates above-average still whites and reds. Several of Hunter's products have won awards for excellence. Cape Mantell is known for its sauvignon blanc; Penfolds and Montana both offer a wide range of varietals, as well as drinkable vin ordinaire (known, because of its container, as "chateau cardboard").

Mo and Graham, or "Sutts," as she calls him, are personal friends with several of the vintners and enjoy taking people around to visit.

In addition to the wine consumed on tours of the wineries, other vintages are sampled during Mo's five-course gourmet dinners. These sumptuous repasts are created using almost exclusively local produce.

"Apart from some of the cheeses, I buy my supplies from merchants and growers in the area. Of course, some things are home-grown," Mo told me.

At Lake Timara Estate, diners might start with smoked salmon and continue on to trout, venison, or boneless leg of lamb stuffed with spinach, mushrooms, and feta cheese. New Zealand's unusual fruits — kiwis, tamarillos, feijoas — usually feature in the dessert, either fresh or baked into a tart. A different wine is served with each course.

Mo, who is a self-taught chef, enjoys creating in the kitchen, and their 4,200-square-foot house can accommodate company, so she and Graham became farm-stay hosts, in spite of the fact that they still have young children at home. However, sons Scott and Simon are tucked away for the night before dinner is served.

The Lake Timara homestead is grand, but the Suttons' personalities are gregarious and informal, and it's easy to feel relaxed around them. It's obvious that they both like entertaining.

"As a matter of fact," Mo said jokingly, "Graham enjoys the guests far more than the sheep and is thinking of selling off the farm."

Joking is something Mo does very well, and the repartee between the former flight attendant and her husband is often hilarious.

The hostess is quite serious, however, about wanting to re-decorate their house, which dates from 1923, in furnishings representative of the era in which it was built. The wallpapers in the guest bedrooms were chosen after considerable research; bed linens, window shades, and curtains match the paper. One spacious room has twin beds, and the other has a double bed and its own large spa bath and shower.

Downstairs, wall paneling of native timber extends through the family room, dining room, and living room. Mo's goal is to create a "home away from home" for visitors, and she's well on her way to doing it.

She starts each day by delivering an early-morning "cuppa" to guest bedrooms; during the day, coffee and tea are available in the kitchen on a help-yourself basis.

Everyone joins in for tennis on the grass courts, which are next to the large, attractive swimming pool. When the weather is right, a barbecue lunch is served outside on the expansive lawn that surrounds the house. A pretty lake, created long ago when power was needed for a nearby flax mill, completes the appealing scene.

At one time, nine gardeners were employed to maintain the grounds around the estate. Today, "Happy Harry" Lloyd handles the ten acres of gardens and trees single-handedly. His good sense of humor adds to the jovial atmosphere at Lake Timara.

Because of Mo's culinary skills, the abundance of nearby wineries, and the personalities involved, guests at this farm stay find it's easy to eat, drink, and be merry.

PORTAGE HOTEL

R.D. 2
Picton, (057) 34-309

■

HOSTS: Thelma ("T") and Graham Cains.

LOCATION: Marlborough Sounds, Kenepuru Sound: eight miles north of Picton, as the crow flies.

CATEGORY: Historic hotel.

ACCOMMODATIONS: Twenty rooms, all with private bath.

RATES: Moderate.

INCLUDED: Room only.

CREDIT CARDS: All major.

The early Maoris, who fished in both the Queen Charlotte and Kenepuru sounds, saved themselves many hours of hard paddling by dragging their canoes over a low saddle in the isthmus that separates the two bodies of water.

European settlers later followed the example of the natives and ported their boats overland when traveling to Picton for supplies. Before long, a farmhouse on the Kenepuru side of the saddle had been turned into a guest house, known simply as "the Portage." For many years, only basic services were offered to those taking the shortcut across the land. However, by 1935, this natural resting place had become a popular destination, and in 1958 the inn was granted a hotel liquor license.

The early Maoris and European settlers wouldn't recognize the modern hotel that now occupies the historic site on the edge of sparkling Kenepuru Sound.

All twenty pine-paneled bedrooms have a balcony and a water view, and each has a private bath (shower, no tub), a television, and coffee and tea facilities. One room has a canopied water bed.

The accommodations are a short distance from the main building, which houses the reception area, a conservatory-style dining room, a large bar, a game lounge, a workout room, a sauna, and a hot tub.

The glass walls and roof of the dining room extend into a grove of trees, giving diners the sensation of being out-of-doors. During the day, the woods are full of song birds. At night spotlights reveal nocturnal animals going about their business. The wood paneling in the dining room is part of the original guest house. It's not surprising, given the hostelry's waterfront location, that the menu leans heavily toward fresh seafood.

The bar resembles the stern of a ship, complete with propeller and rudder, and bears the name *S.S. Portage*. Photos tracing the hotel's history hang on one wall. Nearby, a large fireplace, arches of used brick, and timber paneling contribute to the prevailing pub atmosphere. Hosts Graham and "T" make an effort to meet each guest, whom they say they "would like to know as individuals, not as room numbers." The barman also introduces visitors to each other and provides friendly conversation.

Reaching the Portage is much easier today than it was for the early Maoris. It's thirty-five miles (an hour and a quarter) by fairly good road from Picton, or the hotel will send a minibus across the saddle to pick up passengers who take the thirty-minute Friendship Cruise or water taxi to Torea Bay. Helicopters chartered for the trip can land on the lawn in front of the main building.

Activities at the Portage include fishing, diving, boating, swimming, hiking, golf, tennis, and hunting. House guests are entitled to use canoes, fishing tackle, the heated swimming pool, and the hot tub, sauna, gym, and tennis courts at no extra charge.

Kenepuru Sound is known for large snapper, and fishermen have a choice of surfcasting, renting a dinghy, or joining a commercial launch. The hotel has a fifteen-foot runabout that can be used for admiring the scenery or waterskiing. A nine-hole golf course is a short distance away.

The Portage is popular with sailors (yachties) who anchor in front and flock to its bars and dining room during the Christmas – New Year period. But except for this brief chaotic time, the hotel is a haven for rest and recreation — just as it was for the early Maoris and European settlers.

RAETIHI LODGE

R.D. 2
Picton, (057) 34-300

■

HOSTS: Betty and John Brooks, Pat and Doug Sundholm.
LOCATION: Marlborough Sounds, Kenepuru Sound: ten miles
northwest of Picton, as the crow flies.
CATEGORY: Bed and breakfast inn.
ACCOMMODATIONS: Eighteen rooms, none with
private bath.
RATES: Moderate.
INCLUDED: All meals.
CREDIT CARDS: All major.

Those who are used to life in the fast lane may not be able to
adjust to the peace and tranquility of Raetihi Lodge. The homey
guest house is isolated on the far side of Kenepuru Sound, many
miles from traffic, pollution, and other concerns of the real world.

On the other hand, Raetihi may provide a unique opportunity
for those with harried lifestyles to relax completely in a pristine
and private environment.

In spite of its seclusion, getting to the waterfront lodge is fairly
easy. Most people arrive in the small planes operated by Skyferry,
a Wellington-based company. These flights land at the Nopera
airstrip, and passengers are transported by courtesy car three miles
to the guest house. It's also possible to drive from Picton, although
the fifty-nine-mile trip takes at least two and a half hours. A third
option would be to take the Friendship Cruise from Picton to
Torea Bay and the minibus to the Portage jetty, where new arrivals
are collected by a launch sent out by Raetihi.

The lodge is operated by Betty and John Brooks and their
daughter and son-in-law, Pat and Doug Sundholm. These four
create a warm family atmosphere. Sometimes after dinner John
plays the organ, the chef plays the guitar or ukulele, and those
who choose to do so join in for a sing-along. At other times, guests
get together to play pool, Ping-Pong, board games, or cards.

"At seven-thirty in the morning we roll a cart down the hallway and everyone comes out of their rooms to get a cup of
early-morning tea" Pat told me. "At other places it wouldn't

happen, but here people feel so at home they sometimes stand around in their dressing gowns [bathrobes] discussing the day's agenda."

Often these plans include fishing, waterskiing, cruising, swimming, and hiking. The use of dinghies and canoes is complimentary; power boats can be rented. For the less energetic there are a hot tub, a library, and a bar.

Accommodations at Raetihi Lodge are eighteen comfortable rooms, twelve of which have sinks. The quarters in the Winekere wing are the most spacious and have the advantage of having their own exterior doors. Showers and toilets are spaced around the halls at convenient locations.

In addition to the early-morning tea, the hosts serve breakfast, morning tea, lunch, afternoon tea, dinner, and supper. When I asked Pat if there were coffee and tea facilities, she said, "Yes, if anyone wants more than the seven cups a day we give them."

The meals are country-style, rather than gourmet, which seems appropriate in this rustic setting. Wine is available for those who wish to order it. The specialties of the house are local snapper and chowder made from Kenepuru Sound mussels. Milk and cream come fom the lodge's three cows, and eggs are from its chickens. Picnic lunches can be prepared for those heading out on hikes through the surrounding native woodland or for a long day of fishing.

Raetihi is very popular with families during the New Zealand school holidays, which run from mid-December to the first week in February. Activities are more adult-oriented at other times of the year.

Informality is the key. Guests can get a beer at the bar and enjoy it at the water's edge or on the jetty. Sometimes on long summer evenings, supper is served at picnic tables on the lawn.

Privacy is another key. The Brookses and Sundholms don't serve meals or drinks to anyone but registered guests, and they don't permit sightseers on their property.

Informality? Privacy? Relaxation? Seclusion? As I said, those who are accustomed to life in the fast lane may not be able to adjust to the pace at Raetihi Lodge.

CALIFORNIA HOUSE

29 Collingwood Street
Nelson, (054) 84-173

■

HOSTESS: Carol Glen.

LOCATION: Central Nelson.

CATEGORY: Bed and breakfast inn.

ACCOMMODATIONS: Six rooms, none with private bath.

RATES: Moderate.

INCLUDED: Breakfast, pre-dinner wine with snacks.

CREDIT CARDS: None.

RESTRICTIONS: No smoking; no young children.

Even with a different name this Nelson inn would still be a California house. Its owner, Carol Glen, hails from Mendocino County, and her B & B is a look-alike for those found along the Golden State's northern coast.

Oversized windows and eleven-foot ceilings form the backdrop for interesting period antiques. Imported percale bed linens are included in the spacious guest rooms, as are fresh flowers, doilies, books, and beautiful wallpapers. Twenty-four stained-glass windows, oak paneling, three fireplaces, a sunny verandah, and lovely flower gardens help to complete the old-world scene.

Carol discovered her charming colonial home during a 1981 visit to New Zealand. On the last day of her stay, she went for a walk and noticed a For Sale sign at 29 Collingwood Street. In spite of the fact that it was then a sorry-looking boarding house, Carol was able to see its potential. She hurriedly located an attorney and gave him power to act on her behalf. A few months later, the property was hers, and she began the arduous task of making it livable.

One by one, with the help of a friend, the rooms were renovated. "Margaret's Room" is named after Carol's mother, who made a sizable financial contribution to the project. The "Everett Room" acknowledges the home's original owners. "The Pantry" no longer resembles its former purpose. "Morning Sun" might not be the best room for late risers.

The single-story abode has six company bedrooms, three bathrooms, and a comfortable parlor. The house, which was built in 1893, is registered by the Historic Places Trust.

The inn is renowned for its California-style breakfasts. Some of Carol's favorite treats are fresh orange juice, just-picked berries topped with wonderful New Zealand cream, home-baked apricot nut bread, cheese blintzes, ham and sour cream omelets, Finnish pancakes, and freshly ground coffee. Guests gather around a large wooden table in her sunny kitchen for the morning meal.

My first visit to the B & B was disappointing: the inn was closed, as it is every year from June 15 to September 15. "I can't keep this place warm," Carol later explained, "and I won't have people here if I can't make them comfortable."

Several months later, I returned and found the California House in full swing. The hostess was serving wine and cheese on the verandah, and everyone was discussing their day's activities. Later that evening, a fabulous pumpkin pie appeared in the parlor, and we remembered that it was Thanksgiving.

Carol's other thoughtful extras — turning down beds, putting mints on pillows, leaving a decanter of sherry next to the coffee and tea facilities — don't seem out of the ordinary to veterans of U.S. bed and breakfast inns, but they surprise and delight New Zealanders.

Carol's penchant for teddy bears also amuses Kiwis. I would have loved to see the look on the face of the *New Zealand Woman's Weekly* reporter as the hostess explained that "the bears send out good vibes and pull in the right kind of people."

Carol believes her guests want peace and quiet. "Part of the concept of a California inn is that it's a place where people can converse. That's why I don't have a television or a stereo."

Some visitors may crave tranquility, but I have to confess: it's her pumpkin pie that motivates me to plan a return engagement.

TRAFALGAR GUEST HOUSE

46 Trafalgar Street
Nelson, (054) 83-980

■

HOSTS: Lynn and Jeff Hunter.
LOCATION: Central Nelson.
CATEGORY: Bed and breakfast inn.
ACCOMMODATIONS: Three rooms, none with private bath.
RATES: Inexpensive.
INCLUDED: Breakfast.
CREDIT CARDS: All major.

The central location and reasonable tariffs of the Trafalgar Guest House make it a popular spot with budget-conscious Americans and Canadians. Trafalgar Street is Nelson's main thoroughfare, and the two-story B & B is just a block from the city center. The Newmans bus depot on Hardy Street is less than a ten-minute walk away.

A cooked breakfast of fruit, juice, cereal, bacon, eggs, toast, and tea or coffee is included in the rate. This hearty meal is prepared by Lynn Hunter, who, with her husband Jeff, manages the inn.

The Hunters, who immigrated from Liverpool, do all they can for guests and direct visitors to the main points of interest in the area, which are the Suter Art Gallery, Broadgreen, and the Christ Church Cathedral.

The gallery, which is next to the lovely Queen's Gardens, has an excellent craft shop and a nice restaurant. Broadgreen, a two-story cob house built about 1855, provides a peek into New Zealand's Victorian period. The cathedral looms over the city from a rise at the top of Trafalgar Street.

In spite of the appeal of these attractions, Tahuna Beach remains Nelson's most popular spot. The wide stretch of sand three miles from town is safe for swimming and ideal for jogging.

Another favorite activity is berry picking. Several raspberry and strawberry farms allow people to pick their own delicious fruit during the summer months.

For a look at the rural area east of Nelson, visitors can join the mail carrier as he makes his daily (except Sunday) four-hour trip around the region.

The Hunters will store excess baggage for those who wish to go hiking in Abel Tasman National Park, where the terrain includes crescents of beautiful deserted beach and miles of preserved native bush.

Lynn can also give advice on venues for squash and aerobics, as those are her favorite pastimes.

At Trafalgar Guest House the three guest bedrooms each have their own sinks and share two toilets and one shower. One room has a double bed and a single; the other two rooms have twin beds. The accommodations are homey and clean; a television and coffee and tea facilities are provided in the parlor.

In addition to hiking, berry picking, and sightseeing, many visitors to Nelson are attracted to the town's plethora of pottery shops. The clay is exceptionally good in this area, and, as a result, sixty full-time potters and four hundred hobbyists make their home here. The South Street gallery and Clay Works are only two of the stores that display the work of local artisans.

The most popular dining spot in Nelson is Chez Eelco, an informal BYO restaurant near the cathedral. It looks like a coffee house left over from the Beatnik generation; in this respect, it reflects the fact that Nelson is a community of potters, weavers, and others devoted to an "alternative lifestyle."

Tasman scallops and Marlborough mussels are the specialties at Chez Eelco, but it's also a popular spot for cappuccino, Twinings tea, and bran muffins. It's open every day, and there's sporadic live entertainment.

Chez Eelco, like nearly everything else in town, is an easy walk from the Trafalgar Guest House.

WHITE'S GUEST HOUSE

430 High Street
Motueka, (0524) 87-318

■

HOSTS: Rachael and Laddie White.

LOCATION: Thirty-one miles northwest of Nelson.

CATEGORY: Bed and breakfast inn.

ACCOMMODATIONS: Five rooms, none with private bath.

RATES: Inexpensive.

INCLUDED: Breakfast.

CREDIT CARDS: None.

After my first book on New Zealand was published, I received a letter from Rachael White in which she expressed dismay that "Motueka, surely the gateway to the Golden Bay area, was not even mentioned."

She went on to say, "My husband and I recently opened our twelve-bed guest house. We run a homely [homey] establishment with the personal touch, serve an excellent, satisfying breakfast, and offer evening meals by arrangement."

In my reply to her letter I assured Mrs. White that my omission of Motueka was merely an oversight and that it wouldn't happen again. What I didn't say was that I had once been employed as an orchard worker in her area and my memories of "Mot," as we called it, were not exactly the stuff of travel guidebooks.

However, a promise is a promise, so I went back to "the gateway to Golden Bay" and found that from the tourist's point of view (as opposed to the apple picker's) it is indeed an appealing community.

The town is in the center of a major fruit-, tobacco-, and hops-growing area. Apples and pears (pip fruit) from here are exported to more than forty foreign countries. Large numbers of seasonal workers continue to be employed, but they have now been joined by a year-round population of craftspeople, apparently drawn by the district's equable climate. Wood carvers, wool spinners, weavers, and potters maintain studios and welcome visitors to watch them work.

Not far from Motueka, the Ngarua limestone caves reach into the Marble Mountain of Takaka Hill. The local bus company operates tours to the caves and to some wineries in the area.

Kaiteriteri, eight miles to the north, is well known for its golden-sand beach. It is from here that launch trips depart for the many beautiful bays of Abel Tasman National Park. Passengers can request to be put ashore at lunch time or can stay on the boat as it goes to the north end of the park to service backpackers. The same company that operates the launch, Abel Tasman National Park Enterprises, also conducts four-day guided walks in the park.

Rachael was right. I shouldn't have failed to mention this scenic area. She was also accurate in her description of their B & B.

The five guest rooms have a country look; the quilts and curtains are covered in a small floral pattern. One room has a single bed; three rooms have doubles, and another has one double bed and two singles. Each has a sink, and two bathrooms (showers, no tubs) are shared between the guests.

The large parlor, warmed by a wood-burning stove, is equipped with television, coffee and tea facilities, and shelves full of books.

In addition to breakfast, they serve a light lunch of either soup and toast in the winter or salad in the summer, for about $2. Three-course dinners, which usually include good local fresh fish, cost about $7. (The inn has a BYO license.) Rachael's creative home cooking—especially her apple crumble—is one of the factors that contribute to the success of the B & B.

The other important ingredient is the warm atmosphere generated by the hosts. Laddie, an accountant by profession, helps in any way he can, whether that means picking up new arrivals at the bus station, spreading someone's sleeping bag on the lawn to dry, or scraping the frost off a windshield (windscreen) on a cold morning. They both are qualified to advise hikers (trampers), since they have experience on the nearby trails.

And they are qualified to prompt an errant travel writer—which, happily, they did.

REVINGTON'S

P.O. Box 86, Tainui Street
Greymouth, (027) 7055

■

HOST: Ray Larkin.
LOCATION: Central Greymouth.
CATEGORY: Historic hotel.
ACCOMMODATIONS: Thirty rooms, twenty-six with private bath.
RATES: Inexpensive.
INCLUDED: Room only.
CREDIT CARDS: All major.

The discovery of gold near Greymouth in 1864 started a rush to the previously unpopulated West Coast. A town site was laid out, hotels were built, and a coach route from Christchurch was pushed through Arthur's pass.

One of those frontier hotels was Revington's, a watering hole built fifteen years after the first strike. The property has been tastefully restored and now offers atmospheric accommodations and a lively pub ambiance to travelers.

Each comfortable bedroom has a television, a telephone, and coffee and tea facilities. The majority of rooms have private baths, and Maori legends decorate the walls.

Downstairs, the bars attract an animated local crowd who seem to enjoy socializing with visitors. Many of these folks are involved in the timber business, which has kept the town alive since the demise of gold mining and the coal industry.

A photo in the foyer of the two-story hotel commemorates the 1954 visit of Queen Elizabeth II.

A Cobb and Co restaurant (New Zealand's answer to Denny's) in the hotel provides reasonably priced meals in coffee-shop surroundings. Not far away, Bonzi serves pizza that manager Ray Larkin describes as "brilliant."

Ray makes it a point to greet guests and will even go to the bus or train station to pick up new arrivals.

Eight miles south of Greymouth at Shantytown, visitors can tour a replica of a gold-field town typical of those found on the West Coast in the nineteenth century. The reconstructed gold-buying office, printing shop, stables, store, and jail (gaol) look very much like ones found in similar communities in California. The church, built in 1866, was moved to Shantytown from its original site in No Town.

At Coaltown, a museum sixty-three miles to the north in Westport, excellent displays and audio-visual presentations describe the gold- and coal-mining industries and their effect on the development of the region.

Shantytown and Coaltown are worthwhile attractions, but in my opinion, neither of these places has the appeal of the Punakaiki Pancake Rocks located on the coast twenty-eight miles north of Greymouth. The stratified limestone stacks and the rough seas that constantly pound against them are an awesome sight. Thundering spray jets up through blowholes that have been worn in the cliffs.

The West Coast region (known as "Westland") was purchased from the Maoris by Queen Victoria's government in 1860. The terms were arranged by a young Scot, James Mackay, who was authorized to pay four hundred pounds for the land. The clever Mackay managed to make the purchase for only three hundred pounds, but he nearly drowned in the Grey River as he made his way back to the government offices in Nelson.

The only thanks he received was a letter of reprimand that chastised him for allowing the deed to become water-stained. It is doubly ironic that within a decade this land yielded more than twelve million pounds in gold.

LAKE BRUNNER LODGE

Mitchells, R.D. Kumara
Westland; (027) 80-163

■

HOSTS: Marian van der Goes and Ray Grubb.
LOCATION: Twenty-nine miles southeast of Greymouth.
CATEGORY: Country lodge.
ACCOMMODATIONS: Eight rooms, all with private bath.
RATES: Moderate.
INCLUDED: Room only.
CREDIT CARDS: All major.

Detailed maps of South Island show a "historic fishing lodge" at Mitchells on the west side of Lake Brunner. This description creates a false image of decrepit wooden shacks in various states of collapse.

Yes, there have been accommodations for sportsmen in this location since the late nineteenth century, and the main building at Lake Brunner Lodge is more than fifty years old, but the property was totally renovated in 1986 and now offers the first-class comfort and personal attention associated with the finest country dwellings.

"Our aim is to be the best fishing lodge in New Zealand," said hostess Marian van der Goes. "We've limited ourselves to eight bedrooms, so we can spend time with guests and give the kind of service people want."

The renovations to the 1930s weatherboard structure were designed by Sarah Scott, New Zealand's Architect of the Year for 1984, who preserved the colonial bay windows and verandahs and chose cream with white and green trim for the exterior.

Marian supervised the interior decorating, which includes a restful cream-and-medium-blue color scheme in the bedrooms. Early New Zealand prints, brass lights, and apricot quilts complete the decor. Furniture made of lovely, rich heart rimu is used throughout the single-story building.

Deluxe guest rooms have a lake view, as do the attractive dining room and parlor. One bedroom has an open fireplace. Lest visitors forget the origins of this historic spot, the sleeping quarters are each named after a fishing fly.

Trout and salmon found in Lake Brunner and the nearby rivers and streams continue to lure visitors to the lodge, just as they did more than a hundred years ago. Professional guides and all the necessary equipment are available for both novice and experienced fishermen.

Others can swim beneath a one-hundred-foot waterfall or at the lake front, pan for gold, look for birds while walking in the surrounding native forest, ride horses, or raft rivers. Hunters can be helicoptered to the back country, where red deer, chamois, wild boar, and thar (a Himalayan mountain goat) roam; duck hunting is popular from May to July.

Sporting activities are a big part of the life at Lake Brunner Lodge, but the gourmet game meals that Marian oversees are just as important.

The day starts with either a Continental breakfast of croissants, crumpets, and homemade jam or a cooked meal of bacon, sausages, eggs, tomatoes, and fresh trout (if caught by a guest).

Lunch might be a picnic of French bread, sausages, quiche, fresh fruit, and wine. Dinner could be hare, salmon, wild boar, or any other New Zealand delicacy available. Meals are not included in the tariff. Breakfast costs $4 to $6; lunch is about $8; dinner $19 plus wine.

Lake Brunner Lodge

Before the evening meal, guests gather in the parlor for cocktails and hors d'oeuvres with the hosts. The big log fire and view of the lake and mountains add to the congenial atmosphere in the dining room.

The beauty and solitude of Lake Brunner and its nearly uninhabited surroundings are really special. The only hamlet in the area, Moana, has a wonderful little country pub and less than a hundred residents.

Access to the lodge is by road or train through Arthur's Pass from Christchurch or by air to Hokitika, where Marian and Ray pick up new arrivals.

Unknowing travelers who drive to the spot on the map marked "historic fishing lodge" are in for a big surprise.

CENTRAL GUEST HOUSE

20 Hamilton Street
Hokitika, Hokitika 1232

■

HOSTS: Glenda and Martin Burt.

LOCATION: Twenty-seven miles southwest of Greymouth.

CATEGORY: Bed and breakfast inn.

ACCOMMODATIONS: Seven rooms, none with private bath.

RATES: Inexpensive.

INCLUDED: Room only.

CREDIT CARDS: None.

The Central Guest House is, as the name implies, located very near the center of Hokitika. However, peace and quiet isn't a problem at the B & B, because very little traffic passes by.

Hosts Glenda and Martin Burt go out of their way to accommodate visitors. In the past, this has meant sewing a torn coat, drying out wet tents, and serving a delayed breakfast to late sleepers. They've also considerably remodeled their B & B to provide access and facilities for the handicapped. Martin is an experienced fisherman and has lots of good advice on landing salmon or trout on nearby rivers and lakes. Glenda has information for hikers. Both strongly encourage guests to tour the glowworm caves at the north edge of town.

Clyde and St. Bathans are picturesque relics of the Central Otago gold rush of the 1860s.

THE GOLDFIELD'S INN

41 Frankton Road
Queenstown, (0294) 27-211
■

HOSTS: Jill and Doug Gibson.
LOCATION: Central Queenstown.
CATEGORY: Bed and breakfast inn.
ACCOMMODATIONS: Six rooms, four with private bath.
RATES: Inexpensive.
INCLUDED: Breakfast.
CREDIT CARDS: All major.

Majestic mountains, sparkling water, and clean air give Queenstown the feel of an Alpine village and provide the perfect backdrop for the Swiss-chalet-style buildings of the Goldfield's Inn.

Geraniums grow in flower boxes on the balconies during spring and summer. In winter the cheerful red-roofed structures are sometimes surrounded by snow.

The inn is located on the main road, a ten-minute walk from the center of town. The two rooms in the house have sinks and share other facilities; bedrooms in the detached chalets have private bathrooms (showers, no tubs). Jill and Doug serve a filling Kiwi breakfast in the parlor, where there are also coffee and tea facilities and a television for guests. The property has a magnificent view of Lake Wakatipu and the Remarkables.

The friendly hosts are more than willing to advise visitors on how best to enjoy their area. Jill is an avid golfer and encourages players to try the course at nearby Calvin Heights, which many American guests have told her is one of the most picturesque in the world.

Doug is interested in photography and likes to tell fellow camera buffs where to get picture-postcard shots. Hikers and skiers can store equipment at the inn while pursuing other interests.

The Gibsons don't normally offer lunch and dinner, but "hot

soup and porridge are always available in winter," and they provide dishes and picnic tables during the summer for anyone who wants to have a barbecue dinner.

Because of the hosts' congenial personalities, a warm camaraderie frequently develops among house guests. Sometimes folks who have met over breakfast or in the parlor go out sightseeing together. In the evenings Scrabble is a popular pursuit.

Travelers with rented cars are happy to find off-street parking. For those who are using public transportation, the intercity coach drops off passengers at the Goldfield's gate, as does the airport bus.

Many sights and dining spots are within walking distance of the B & B. The *Earnslaw*, a veteran steamship that cruises the lake, leaves from the wharf near Beach Street. The gondola to Bob's Peak and the Skyline Restaurant departs from its station at the end of Brecon Street. No one should miss the spectacular view over town, lake, and mountains provided by the four-seater bubble cars. Near the gondola station, the Queenstown Motor Museum houses a large display of vintage cars.

The meals in the Skyline Restaurant are good, but the Cow remains my favorite eating spot in town. Located on Cow Lane in a tiny, rustic building, the popular BYO is crowded almost every night of the year. The menu includes good pasta and world-class pizza. Because there are only five booths, diners wait their turn by the open fire and sharing tables is de rigueur.

Those who are too hungry to wait for pizza can pick up fish and chips at the Town Fish Shop and dine at one of the picnic tables back at Goldfield's.

Their view is such that even humble food will seem like a regal repast.

HULBERT HOUSE

68 Ballarat Street
Queenstown; (0294) 28-767

■

HOST: Ted Sturt.
LOCATION: Central Queenstown.
CATEGORY: Bed and breakfast inn.
ACCOMMODATIONS: Five rooms, all with private bath.
RATES: Moderate.
INCLUDED: Breakfast.
CREDIT CARDS: All major.

Ted Sturt had his work cut out for him when he purchased Hulbert House in 1981. The seventeen-room colonial villa had been sadly neglected in its later years and contained, according to the host, "a lot of modern rubbish."

It seems ironic that this former British army captain and mechanical engineer went to Queenstown intending to pursue the glamorous life of a ski instructor, but fell in love with the derelict mansion and ended up working on its restoration from dawn to dusk seven days a week.

"Some nights I went to bed exhausted, wondering just what I'd taken on," Ted confided. "And in order to finance the project, I sold my car, my watch, and my television."

The Victorian "gentleman's residence" was built in 1889 for Horatio Nelson Firth, a senior court official, and his wife, Catherine Mary O'Sullivan. The Firths, who lived in the house with their six children and servants, entertained in the grand manner until a change in their financial fortune occurred around the turn of the century.

In 1901 Mrs. Firth advertised Hulbert House as a guest house and was said to "provide accommodation of the first order." The family sold the property in 1910, and it has subsequently been used as a nursing home, a private girls' school, a maternity hospital, and a staff hostel.

Ted was able to locate the original architects' building plans, to which he referred throughout the restoration. Some large rooms had been divided into smaller ones over the years, but they are now pretty much back to their original dimensions, and the villa has been registered with the Historic Places Trust.

Five spacious bedrooms, three with en suite bathrooms and two with detached baths, now await house guests. The attractive rooms are furnished in antiques, some belonging to Ted and others on loan from friends. A few pieces, like the kauri coal bin (locker) that supports a bedside light, are original to the house.

In the Governor's Room, named for Ted's friend the former governor general Sir David Beattie, a campaign chest used by colonists serves as a bureau. This grand bedchamber has two large bay windows, a beautiful ornamental plaster ceiling, one queen-sized bed, and one single. Like many rooms in the inn, the Governor's enjoys a fabulous town and lake view.

In the parlor Ted has tastefully drawn the color scheme from the pale green and rose Italian tiles that surround the fireplace; wall coverings, uphostery, and draperies are appropriately coordinated. Throughout the B & B, bowls of potpourri lightly scent the air.

Five working fireplaces remain in the house. One of these is in the dining room, where guests gather around a solid kauri table for breakfast. The meal starts with fruit, either fresh or preserved, and continues on to bacon and eggs, cereals, Twinings teas, freshly ground coffee, toasted whole-grain bread, and four kinds of imported marmalade — the latter being evidence of the host's British background.

Many VIPs have stayed at Hulbert House, including the

Hulbert House

governor general's wife, Lady Beattie, but Ted didn't change his routine for them, because all of his company receives the same courteous treatment and the best personal service possible. Beds are turned down at night, and in the winter electric blankets are preheated. Housemaids tiptoe into rooms several times a day to put out fresh towels and tidy up.

Ted is maintaining the standards set by Mrs. Firth more than eighty-five years ago by "providing accommodation of the first order in Queenstown" and being "most attentive to the requirements of visitors."

Because of Ted, Hulbert House is once again a "gentleman's residence."

HOME STAY MAY

Lake Hayes, R.D. 2
Queenstown; (029420) 430
■

HOSTS: Clarice and Bill May.

LOCATION: Nine miles northeast of Queenstown.

CATEGORY: Home stay.

ACCOMMODATIONS: Three rooms, none with private bath.

RATES: Moderate.

INCLUDED: Breakfast.

CREDIT CARDS: None.

It's hard to say what's most impressive about Home Stay May. The view over Lake Hayes is a knockout, but Clarice and Bill's hospitality is some of the warmest in the country. When I read their visitors' book, I realized I wasn't the only person who felt slightly awed by the situation. Comments about "the marvelous Mays" included "The setting is exceeded only by your hospitality" and "Perfect hosts in a perfect setting."

The Maoris called Lake Hayes *Wai-whaka-ata*, which means "water that reflects objects," because its clear blue surface often mirrors its surroundings. The lake, which is fringed by trees, is one of the prettiest in the South Island.

The Mays' two-story house sits on a knoll with an unobstructed water view from most rooms, including two of the three guest bedrooms.

Bill and Clarice moved to this idyllic spot when they retired from farming in 1980, and neither of them lost any time getting involved in community activities. Bill is a member of the Rotary, and he's happy to take visiting Rotarians with him to their Tuesday meetings in Queenstown. Clarice, who is a retired nurse, received the Queen's Service Medal for her extensive hospital volunteer work. Her other hobbies include sewing, patchwork, and cooking.

The person who wrote in the guest book, "My stomach thanks you for the wonderful food; my heart thanks you for your warm hospitality" was obviously as impressed with Clarice's cuisine as I was.

The house breakfast specialty is bran muffins made with yogurt and bananas and served with lots of perked coffee. Three-course dinners, which are available for an extra $14 (including wine), often include homemade onion soup, freshly baked bread, roast venison or lamb, and pavlova.

Clarice, a talented gardener, maintains a hothouse (glass house) where tomatoes, lettuce, and cucumbers are grown. She also has "a proper old English garden" that boasts some beautiful roses.

The Mays enjoy taking visitors to see Mayfield, the family farm their son took over when they retired. Bill's ancestors began farming on this land in 1863, and he's understandably proud of the fact that his property won an award for being the best-managed farm in Southland nine years in a row.

Clarice and Bill have plenty of free time to spend with guests. They take people sightseeing for a slight extra charge.

Many house guests welcome the chance to relax and get caught up on laundry and postcards in the Mays' cozy waterfront home. In spite of the fact that none of their five children or eight grandchildren live with them, the house has a strong family atmosphere.

One upstairs double room with a patchwork motif shares a bathroom with the hosts. Downstairs, a room with twin beds and a room with one single bed share a bathroom.

The Mays seem to have perfected the art of making folks feel welcome. They fly the flag of overseas visitors, and they go out of their way to meet any special requests.

Savvy travelers will follow my lead and express a wish that "bumblebees" be served with afternoon tea.

TWENTY WILTSHIRE STREET

20 Wiltshire Street
Arrowtown, (029420) 326

■

HOSTESS: Cynthia Balfour.

LOCATION: Twelve miles northeast of Queenstown.

CATEGORY: Home stay.

ACCOMMODATIONS: Two rooms share one bath.

RATES: Moderate.

INCLUDED: Breakfast.

CREDIT CARDS: None.

The eclectic decor of Cynthia Balfour's Arrowtown cottage reflects the hostess's various interests and travel experiences. Paintings of Canadian scenes hanging throughout the house are souvenirs from the seventeen years she lived in Calgary while pursuing a career in public relations. Before that she worked in London for five years and in a guest house in Scotland for two summers.

The cache of cookbooks stored in a kitchen cupboard represent a myriad of ethnic cuisines. Cooking is one of Cynthia's hobbies, and she enjoys preparing a range of international dishes as well as traditional New Zealand fare. (Breakfast is included in her home-stay tariff, and dinner is available for an extra charge of $11, including wine.)

The dining room furniture is Danish modern; the downstairs bedroom has a lovely antique dresser and a cane headboard. In the cozy upstairs room, guests sleep in twin beds under open-beam ceilings and a pair of dormer windows.

Gardening is another of Cynthia's interests. Beautiful geraniums bloom in the glass conservatory near the kitchen; outside, roses and a rock garden border the lawn.

The hostess welcomes new arrivals to her attractive home with a cup of coffee or tea and a home-baked treat served near the red-brick fireplace hearth in the living room. Her two Canadian cats, brought to New Zealand after being quarantined in England, pay little heed to visitors.

Cynthia, on the other hand, takes a personal interest in her guests and enjoys introducing them to Arrowtown. Travelers who stay with her in the latter part of April can attend the Autumn Festival, which includes dancing in the street, a busker's carnival, a barbershop quartet competition, and the Miner's Hop.

From July to September, skiing is the hostess's principal pastime, and house guests, who are welcome to ride to and from the slopes with her, get the added benefit of her extensive experience on the local mountains.

At any time of the year Cynthia will collect people from the coach depot or airport in Queenstown, although there is a daily bus to Arrowtown.

Wiltshire Street is close to the center of town, where shops and a good museum are housed in buildings whose façades are indicative of the area's history. The settlement flourished during the gold rush of the 1860s but barely existed as a farming community after that. More recently, it has become a mecca for tourists who are drawn by the picturesque mining cottages, beautiful deciduous trees, and surrounding mountain ranges.

The Stone Cottage, a wonderful little cafe in which Cynthia was once a partner, specializes in delicious Devonshire cream teas. At lunch time they also serve homemade soup, quiche, casseroles, and sandwiches.

The Flower Barn, located a mile or two out of town, is also well worth a visit for those who might like to buy some Kiwi potpourri or dried flowers to take home. As anyone who's been to Twenty Wiltshire Street would agree, decorative reminders of past journeys add a special warmth to a house and help to extend travel memories.

RIVER BANK FARM

P.O. Box 203
Wanaka, (02943) 7968

■

HOSTS: Judy and Jonathan Elworthy.

LOCATION: Sixty-nine miles northeast of Queenstown.

CATEGORY: Farm stay.

ACCOMMODATIONS: Two rooms share one bath.

RATES: Moderately expensive.

INCLUDED: All meals, wine with dinner.

CREDIT CARDS: None.

River Bank Farm is not a typical farm stay, and Judy and Jonathan Elworthy are not average Kiwi farmers.

To begin with, their property consists of only twenty acres, and it's occupied by vegetables and trees — not sheep. And instead of a white weatherboard colonial homestead, the Elworthys reside in a modern ranch-style house.

However, Jonathan knows a lot about farming; in 1860 his great-grandfather founded Craigmore Station, one of the largest and most successful in the South Island. The station is still owned by Elworthys, but Jonathan chose a career in politics instead of agriculture and for ten years was a member of Parliament.

His experience in the government makes River Bank Farm a good spot for anyone who enjoys talking about current events, and because he was Minister of Lands and Forests, this is also an ideal place for people who are interested in hiking and climbing.

The energetic host knows how to get off the beaten path and find little-known beauty spots within the national parks, and he happily accompanies guests on backpacking excursions. Fiordland and Mount Aspiring National Parks, two of New Zealand's best, are nearby, and overnight accommodations in Forest Service huts can be arranged.

Whether outdoors or at home, the Elworthys are wonderful, relaxed people with a good sense of humor. When I asked Judy what sort of meals she likes to prepare, she replied, "Well, we do a cunning wok."

She then went on to explain that they've traveled in China and India and that Mandarin and Tandoori dishes are some of their favorites. "However," she added, "we also love spaghetti Bolognese."

On my last visit to River Bank Farm, Judy served whitebait fritters for lunch and although I don't usually care for these patties of tiny fish, I had to admit they were good.

In addition to her culinary talents, Judy is a violist with the local orchestra, and she plays "a brilliant game of Scrabble."

Both Elworthys are very enthusiastic about the area in which they live and like to show it off to visitors. They take house guests to see the largest deer farm in the country and encourage those who are interested to try waterskiing or windsurfing on Lake Wanaka. Jonathan, who was a pilot in the air force, also enjoys taking guests flying in a Tiger Moth. He's an enthusiastic skier, and there are four "ski fields" in the area (Treble Cone, Cardrona, the Remarkables, and Coronet Peak), plus heli-skiing in the Harris Mountains. Wanaka has a golf course, and fishermen have a choice of three rivers or the lake.

The Elworthy home has two guest bedrooms, one with a double bed and another with twins, and a bathroom used just by company. The house is comfortably furnished and commands a superb mountain view, but its greatest assets are its proprietors.

Judy and Jonathan are not presently involved in politics, but New Zealand couldn't ask for better ambassadors.

WANAKA LODGE

117 Lakeside Road, P.O. Box 48
Wanaka, (02943) 7837
■

HOSTS: Gaye and Ron Brown.
LOCATION: Seventy-two miles northeast of Queenstown.
CATEGORY: Bed and breakfast inn.
ACCOMMODATIONS: Nine rooms, four with private bath.
RATES: Inexpensive.
INCLUDED: Room only.
CREDIT CARDS: All major.

Where do New Zealanders go when they vacation in their own country? Many head for Lake Wanaka and its neighbor Lake

Hawea. These shining blue bodies of water and the alpine peaks that surround them attract water-sports enthusiasts in summer and skiers in winter. However, it's in autumn, when the poplars and willows around the lakes change colors, that the area is really at its best.

The beauty of the lake is framed perfectly by the large picture window in the parlor of Wanaka Lodge. I wasn't surprised when host Ron Brown said, "Some of our guests just sit and watch the view for hours."

Others go walking or fishing, and some try their hand at waterskiing, parasailing, or windsurfing.

The Browns offer "fair dinkum Kiwi hospitality," which includes providing courtesy-car transportation, arranging sightseeing and local activities, and cooking any salmon or trout caught by guests. They'll also help out with onward travel reservations.

Ron prides himself on knowing "what's good value for money" in the area and steers his visitors in this direction. He also gives advice on practical matters, like winter road conditions, and suggests that Highway 89 over the Crown Range from Queenstown be avoided. (Wanaka is forty-two miles from Queenstown via Highway 89 and seventy-two miles via Cromwell, but the shorter route is so dangerous that many rental car companies prohibit its use.)

As an alternative to driving, Wanaka can be reached by air (Newmans) and intercity coach (Road Services). The little township (pop. 1,100) sits at the southern end of the lake, and the B & B is about a half-mile away overlooking Roys Bay. The Mount Aspiring National Park headquarters are in Wanaka, and the Penbroke Village Mall houses some cute shops.

Wanaka Lodge attracts an international clientele who find the inexpensive tariffs and friendly service appealing. This is especially true during the winter months, when the Browns offer a special bed-and-breakfast rate for skiers on a multishare basis.

Four of the nine bedrooms have attached baths, and the others have their own hand basins and share showers and toilets. The decor isn't fancy, but the B & B is maintained in spotless condition. All rooms have heaters and coffee and tea facilities, and the quarters with private baths also have televisions. Everyone is welcome to use the hot tub and watch TV in the parlor.

Meals aren't included in the rate, but breakfast is available for an extra $2 to $4, and four-course dinners are served for $14. The inn has a BYO license and is popular with people staying in other places, as well as house guests.

During the slightly chaotic Christmas–New Year period, when Wanaka is crowded with vacationing New Zealanders, prospective diners would be wise to make reservations ahead of time. At other times of the year, the dining room, the lodge, and the lake can all be enjoyed in relative peace and quiet.

GLENORCHY HOTEL

Glenorchy
Lake Wakatipu, (0294) 29-902
∎

HOSTS: Esther and Oscar Batchelor.
LOCATION: Twenty-six miles northwest of Queenstown.
CATEGORY: Historic hotel.
ACCOMMODATIONS: Seven rooms, four with private bath.
RATES: Inexpensive.
INCLUDED: Room only.
CREDIT CARDS: All major.

To describe the Glenorchy Hotel as being "off the beaten path" would be a gross understatement. The drive from Queenstown along the west arm of Lake Wakatipu takes nearly an hour and is, for the most part, unpaved (not tar-sealed). The hotel is one of the few buildings in the "town" of Glenorchy, which is really just a settlement of less than a hundred people.

Because of its isolation, the little outpost hostelry appeals to travelers who are seeking unspoiled scenic beauty, wilderness hiking, hunting and fishing, and a rustic country-pub experience.

The road to Glenorchy provides fabulous views of blue and green water, sometimes on shore level and at other times from high above. Majestic peaks form a backdrop for remote farms, and worn signposts indicate where tracks lead off to inland lakes and hidden valleys. Regular bus service is available for those without cars.

The old store in Glenorchy was once a cookhouse for early sheepmen, and during World War II the village was a center for scheelite miners. Today, it's a rest and reprovisioning base for hikers on the Routeburn, Rees, Dart, and Greenstone trails (tracks). A ranger for Mount Aspiring National Park is stationed in the community. Fishermen also center themselves in the village and set out each day to catch rainbow and brown trout and Quinet salmon in nearby lakes and rivers.

The hotel is casual enough to allow sportsmen to feel comfortable, and nice enough to appeal to nonsporting travelers.

"We are isolated, small, and homely [homey]," states the brochure.

Four of the seven bedrooms have been upgraded to include attached baths. The other three have sinks and share two bathrooms. Four rooms are furnished with twin beds, and three are triples. The decor is simple but attractive.

The "Great meals!!!" mentioned in the brochure refers to satisfying bacon and eggs breakfasts ($3.50) and hearty lunches ($5) and dinners ($9). Salad and cold cuts typically are served at noon during the summer, with savory stews taking over in the winter. Dinner menus tend toward roasts—beef, lamb, or chicken—and steaks and chops. A choice of home-cooked desserts tops off the meals, which are served in a cheerful little dining room.

The ranch-style hotel, which was built in 1966, also has a guests' parlor with a cozy stone fireplace and comfortable sofas. Visitors use this room to relax with a book or appreciate the mountain scenery through large picture windows.

Drinks are served in the guests' parlor, but the public bar is usually where the livelier crowd congregates. Fishermen, still dressed in bush shirts and gum boots, swap stories; hikers treat themselves to a well-deserved beer. In winter the rustic room is warmed by a potbelly stove.

Sometimes at night Oscar plays the guitar, Esther sings country-western tunes, and the various bar patrons join in.

This country-pub experience, together with the magnificent scenery and wilderness opportunities, makes wandering off the beaten path to the Glenorchy Hotel well worthwhile.

BIRCH HILL

P.O. Box 1
Garston, Southland, (02283) 816

■

HOSTS: Alison and Max Naylor.

LOCATION: Forty-seven miles south of Queenstown.

CATEGORY: Farm stay.

ACCOMMODATIONS: Two rooms share one bath.

RATES: Moderately expensive.

INCLUDED: All meals, wine with dinner.

CREDIT CARDS: None.

Visitors who haven't heard of the Kingston Flyer before arriving at Birch Hill can learn all about the elegant steam train from Max Naylor. The host is one of the train's owners and, with his partners, was responsible for bringing it out of retirement and restoring the vintage rolling stock.

Several times a day, the Kingston Flyer makes the round trip from its station at Kingston to Fairlight. The train is hauled by a coal-fired locomotive that was designed by New Zealand Railways engineers in 1915. Devonshire cream teas are served on board by local women clad in period costumes.

The Flyer earned its name at the turn of the century by making good time on its regular route between Gore, Lumsden, and Kingston, but now that its passengers are tourists wishing to savor the steam age (and afternoon tea), it moves more graciously along the track.

A trip on the Kingston Flyer isn't mandatory for guests at Birch Hill. The farm carries 2,500 Romney sheep on its seven hundred acres, and I, for one, was more interested in learning about farm activities, so Alison loaned me a pair of gum boots and sent me out with their manager. We "fed out" hay to sheep in several "paddocks," and afterwards I watched while he cleaned a ram's hooves and sheared a few ewes. I found out what a "wool press" is and generally gained an appreciation for how hard Kiwi farmers work.

The Naylors have been doing home hosting since 1978 and claim to have been "well trained by the guests." Perked coffee is available for the benefit of American visitors, but otherwise Alison prepares traditional New Zealand dishes.

Roast lamb with fresh vegetables is usually the main course at dinner, and pavlova is often served for dessert. Meals are accompanied by premium domestic wines.

"The finest table in the Southern Hemisphere," one person wrote in the visitors' book, referring to the good food served at Birch Hill. And Max, patting his stomach, added, "I'm wearing Alison's specialties."

The hostess enjoys using local produce. Stewed tamarillos are sometimes served for breakfast; seafood crepes or salmon pâté might be the first course at dinner. Invariably, when zucchini soup is featured at lunch, the recipe is requested.

Alison happily writes out recipes, and she's also very accommodating about other wishes. Those who are interested in spinning and weaving are taken to visit the local expert. Others might like to tour Garston School, which has two classes and a total of thirty-six students.

Fishing can be arranged on the Mataura River, where the brown trout average eighteen to twenty inches. "The water is so clear you fish the fish, not the stream," Max assured me.

The Naylors' boys, Andrew, Timothy, and Paul, are away at school most of the year, but the house still has a welcoming family atmosphere. Two rooms with twin beds and one attractive bathroom are available for company. Pre-dinner drinks are served in the living room, made elegant by brocade wallpaper, an Edwardian couch, and a beautiful ornamental plaster ceiling.

The Naylors collect new arrivals from the bus depot in Garston and, for an extra charge, will also pick up from the airport in Queenstown.

And visitors who wish to ride the Kingston Flyer can be sure that the hosts will happily drive them to the station.

FARM STAY ROBINS

R.D. 1
Te Anau, (02295) 583
■

HOSTS: Karen and Sam Robins.
LOCATION: One hundred miles southwest of Queenstown.
CATEGORY: Farm stay.
ACCOMMODATIONS: Two rooms, none with private bath.
RATES: Moderate.
INCLUDED: Breakfast, dinner, and wine with dinner.
CREDIT CARDS: None.

When I visited Karen and Sam, they were still undecided as to what to name their property. He favored "Titiroa," which is the name of one of the legendary seven great canoes that brought the first Maoris to New Zealand. Karen felt strongly that the farm should be called "The Bridles." When her husband went outside, Karen would assure me that the name was "The Bridles." When Karen left the room, Sam would seem just as convinced about "Titiroa." By the end of the afternoon, my notes looked like chicken scratchings and I had decided that, rather than take sides, I'd simply label their property "Farm Stay Robins."

Regardless of its title, the farm is a pleasant stopover for those who are traveling to or from Te Anau and the wonders of Fiordland. The single-story house affords a view of the Southern Alps to one side and the Takitimu Mountains to the other. Karen and Sam are a nice young couple who treat their guests "as they would good friends."

Like many Kiwi farmers, the Robinses have diversified and now run sheep, cattle, and deer on their 611-acre property. Sam enjoys giving tours, explaining his routines, and demonstrating sheep shearing.

For many years deer were considered noxious animals in New Zealand because they ate the ground cover in sloping forested areas, causing serious erosion problems. The English settlers who introduced the animals apparently gave little thought to the damage they could do. Without any natural predators, the deer population grew out of control, and the government hired professional hunters to cull the herds.

However, by the mid-1960s, the export value of these "pests" was becoming apparent, and after the animals in the accessible areas had been decimated by hunters using helicopters, breeding them on farms became the trend. The popularity of venison and of an aphrodisiac made from antler velvet makes deer a valuable export-dollar earner for New Zealand farmers. The industry has grown to the point where more than 100,000 deer live in farm herds on more than 1,300 Kiwi properties.

Karen and Sam showed me some velvet they were keeping frozen pending exportation. They also introduced me to fruit wines made at a small nearby settlement, the Key. The drink, made from cherries, apricots, plums, raspberries, boysenberries, or elderberries, was sweet and very different from anything I'd ever tasted.

The hosts serve these fruit wines with their home-style two-course dinners. A hearty breakfast is also included in the tariff. Lunch isn't usually offered because visitors are out during the day touring Fiordland attractions (Te Anau is twenty-three miles to the northwest).

Guests are accommodated in attractive bedrooms (one with twin beds and one with a double) and share the bathroom with Karen and Sam. The modern house is decorated in contemporary furnishings, with the exception of an antique Wiesner piano. The fabulous old piece was made in Berlin and has brass candelabras attached on its front side.

After seeing this beautiful instrument, I was surprised to learn that neither of the Robinses is a dedicated musician. Instead, Sam is very interested in sports and would be happy to discuss cricket or rugby with visitors. Horses are Karen's hobby, and house guests are welcome to join her for a ride.

Horseback riding and talking about sports are nearly as much fun as listening to the likable hosts banter cheerfully about a name for their farm.

MARAMA HOUSE

30 Quinton Drive, P.O. Box 239
Te Anau, (0229) 7090

■

HOSTS: Joan and David Croucher.

LOCATION: Fiordland, 112 miles southwest of Queenstown.

CATEGORY: Home stay.

ACCOMMODATIONS: Two rooms share one bath.

RATES: Inexpensive.

INCLUDED: Breakfast.

CREDIT CARDS: None.

Fiordland is a region in the southwest corner of the South Island. It is mainly comprised of Fiordland National Park (New Zealand's largest) and gets its name from the spectacular fingerlike fiords that project into the coast. Milford Sound is the best-known of these inlets.

Other beauty spots in the area are Doubtful Sound, Lake Manapouri, Lake Te Anau, and Sutherland Falls. The terrain is rugged and road access is limited, but not as limited as it was before the completion of the Homer Tunnel in 1953. Three famous hiking trails (the Milford Track, the Routeburn Track, and the Hollyford Valley Walk) make it possible for able-bodied visitors to see some of the most beautiful scenery in the country.

Marama House is a good base for travelers who want to explore and gain an understanding of Fiordland. A mural etched into the window that separates the living room from the kitchen depicts life in the area: deer, backpackers (trampers), fish, kiwis, waterfalls. The large stone fireplace in the living room is made of rock from the excavation of the Homer Tunnel.

Joan and David's house is located only a five-minute walk from the center of Te Anau, the small township (pop. 2,400) that serves as a base for Fiordland excursions. The hosts will pick up new arrivals at Fiordland Travel, which is where the intercity bus stops, or the town terminal of either Mount Cook Airlines or Newmans Air.

Two attractive bedrooms and one bathroom at Marama House are reserved for company. The twin room has a sink, and both rooms have sunny exposures. The two-story home, built in 1961, has open-beam ceilings and large picture windows that capture the view of the surrounding mountains.

The antique cedar and mahogany sideboard in the dining room once belonged to David's grandmother and was brought to New Zealand by his family when they immigrated from the Channel Islands in 1959.

The Crouchers' interest in natural foods is evident in the Continental breakfast they serve to guests. Homemade whole-wheat bread is accompanied by natural fuit juice, fresh fruit, and cereal. The hosts are happy to serve breakfast in bed on request.

Lunch isn't offered, but house guests may use the family's kitchen to prepare something for themselves if they wish. Dinner, when it's available, is often a casual barbecue in the garden. The Crouchers' teen-age sons, Clay and Chad, usually join in at these meals.

Joan is an avid gardener and maintains attactive flower beds, as well as vegetable plots. Dave is a builder, and both hosts enjoy boating, hiking, and spending time with their visitors. The atmosphere at this home stay is relaxed and comfortable. If someone in the family or one of the guests has a lucky day fishing, Fiordland trout and all the trimmings might just be served for dinner.

MATAI TRAVEL LODGE

Mokonui Street
Te Anau, (0229) 7360

HOSTESS: Marilyn Redfern.
LOCATION: Fiordland, 112 miles southwest of Queenstown.
CATEGORY: Bed and breakfast inn.
ACCOMMODATIONS: Seven rooms, none with private bath.
RATES: Moderate.
INCLUDED: Breakfast.
CREDIT CARDS: All major.

It was a dramatic career change, but Marilyn Redfern, a former video editor with Television New Zealand, seems to have adjusted nicely to her new role as B & B hostess. As a matter of fact, she seems to be thriving on it.

In 1986, after nineteen years with TVNZ in Dunedin, Marilyn returned to Te Anau, where she was raised, and bought the Matai Travel Lodge. She brought with her a special warmth and friendliness that have helped to make the inn a popular spot.

Marilyn picks up new arrivals at Fiordland Travel. She makes a point of introducing visitors to each other and enjoys sitting by the fire chatting with her house guests. It's no wonder that the Matai Travel Lodge has a homey, family atmosphere.

The hostess will also try to provide special food for people with a restricted diet. And for those who like hearty Kiwi fare, she prepares a three-course dinner for an extra charge of about $6. These meals usually include soup, roast chicken or lamb, and vegetables. Her specialty dessert is steamed ginger pudding with ice cream.

Marilyn serves a large, filling breakfast because most guests are out sightseeing all day (she'll pack a lunch for an additional $2.50). One of the most popular excursions is to Milford Sound, where Mitre Peak towers over the majestic fiord. Boat trips carry visitors past sheer cliffs that rise to a height of several thousand feet and waterfalls that spill from mountain-locked lakes.

Another popular day trip goes to Doubtful Sound via Lake Manapouri and the West Arm hydroelectric power station. Passengers on the Te Ana-au Caves trip tour limestone caverns and glowworm grottos on the edge of Lake Te Anau.

At the end of the day, Marilyn's guests are happy to return to the bright and airy bedrooms at their Te Anau home-away-from-home. Quaint floral bedspreads and wallpapers contribute to the cozy atmosphere, and all rooms are equipped with sinks.

The original part of the B & B was constructed in the 1930s in the area of the Homer Tunnel and was used as housing for engineers who were building the Milford Road. The cottage was moved to Te Anau after the road was completed and became a workingmen's boarding house. It was converted to a B & B in the mid-1970s.

It's easy to see from the world map in the television room, where former guests have indicated their hometowns with colored pins, that the Matai attracts an international clientele. And it's evident that Marilyn enjoys all her guests and seems especially pleased when former strangers team up for touring or dining out.

December to March is the best time for traveling in Fiordland, during the low season, reduced B & B rates go into effect, but sightseeing excursions operate less frequently.

Some things may be seasonal, but, happily for her house guests, Marilyn's sunny disposition is the same year-round.

DUNSTAN HOUSE

29 Sunderland Street
Clyde; (029442) 555
■

HOSTS: Sue and Ray Blake.
LOCATION: Fifty miles southeast of Queenstown.
CATEGORY: Bed and breakfast inn.
ACCOMMODATIONS: Nine rooms, none with private bath.
RATES: Inexpensive.
INCLUDED: Breakfast.
CREDIT CARDS: All major.
RESTRICTIONS: No children.

It's been more than a hundred years since dancing girls and a brass band entertained at the Dunstan Hotel on Saturday nights, but visitors who stay at this historic inn still come away with a sense of what the old pub must have been like in its heyday.

After gold was discovered in Clyde in 1862, a town sprang up to meet the needs of the miners who flocked to the area. The Dunstan Hotel occupied an integral place in the main street and was surrounded by stables, a general store, a smithy, a billiard room, a barbershop, and a boot shop.

Sue and Ray Blake have restored the hostelry and given it modern comforts while preserving the old-world charm. Their nine bedrooms are furnished with brass beds and antique dressers and armoires. Wood paneling on walls, ceilings, and floors helps to create a cozy feel, as do the stained-glass window and the elaborate banister on the stairway leading up to the second floor. In the dining room a collection of interesting old bottles and antique teapots is on display.

The hosts have also restored the personal service associated with nineteenth-century hotels: Early-morning tea and a newspaper are delivered to guests in bed. Shoes left outside bedroom doors are polished during the night. And on chilly mornings a roaring fire warms diners while they enjoy an English-style breakfast.

The contemporary services are there, too. Sue and Ray will pick up new arrivals at the airport or bus depot (Mount Cook flies into nearby Alexandra). Tea- and coffee-making facilities and cookies (bickies) are provided in the sitting room. Transportation to the four ski areas within an hour's drive of Clyde is provided at an extra charge. Reduced winter-season tariffs are offered.

The original hotel was an overnight stop for the Cobb and Co coaches that carried passengers from Dunedin to the gold-field settlements. At that time, separate parlors were used by ladies and gentlemen. Today, guests are more likely to sit in the comfortable wicker furniture on the second-story verandah and enjoy the view of the surrounding Central Otago hills.

More energetic visitors hike along old coach trails and explore the caves where Chinese workers lived.

Across the street from Dunstan House, a collection of single-story schist cottages have been converted into craft shops and small stores. The buildings face into a courtyard dotted with large walnut trees and picnic tables.

At the corner of the marketplace, Olivers Restaurant offers gourmet cuisine in a warm atmosphere created by huge stone fireplaces, candelabras glowing on the mantle, a good wine cellar, and caring service.

The restaurant is housed in the general store for miners built in 1862 by Mr. Benjamin Naylor. By 1870, the industrious English immigrant was well established in his handsome stone building, and a sign proclaiming him "Wine Spirit Merchant, General Storekeeper" was displayed over the door.

The old sign was preserved when the property was reopened as Olivers Restaurant in 1977 by Fleur Sullivan and John Braine. This amiable couple have devised a menu as appealing as their cozy ambiance. Creative dishes abound. An appetizer of mushrooms and bacon might be followed by a first course of kidney stroganoff or oyster kebab with hollandaise. Loin of pork grilled with sesame seeds, seafood pasta with crayfish and scampi, and fillet steak topped with pickled walnuts are typical entrées.

In 1984, the year in which the Courtyard and Marketplace opened, the restaurant won the Tourism Design Award. It has also received awards from the New Zealand Historic Places Trust and the David Cox Foundation.

It's not surprising that Sue and Ray Blake are good friends with Fleur and John. Both couples seem equally dedicated to preserving the old-world charm of their properties and to providing gracious hospitality to travelers.

VULCAN HOTEL

R.D. 1 Oturehua
St. Bathans, Central Otago, Omakau 629
■

HOSTS: Wendy and Bruce Blakie.
LOCATION: Nine-two miles northeast of Queenstown.
CATEGORY: Historic hotel.
ACCOMMODATIONS: Three rooms, none with private bath.
RATES: Inexpensive.
INCLUDED: Breakfast.
CREDIT CARDS: None.

During the Central Otago gold rush, St. Bathans had more than a thousand residents and thirteen pubs. Today, the Vulcan Hotel, the sole survivor, stands alone in the tiny hamlet with a permanent population of about twenty-five.

The town is a favorite of New Zealanders (overseas visitors don't normally venture this far off the beaten path) who come to look at the historic buildings, have a drink (or two) in the atmospheric pub, and participate in water sports on adjacent Blue Lake.

The single-story mud-brick hotel was built around 1863 and occupies a prominent position in the main street. Most of the nearby buildings are deserted, but they are of interest because of their classic period architecture. The simple iron Anglican church has been restored, as have the public hall and post office.

The church was sent out from London "prefabricated . . . complete in every respect" as a replacement for the original one, which was destroyed in a gale the day after it was formally opened in 1865. Exhibits displayed in the mail room of the post office illustrate the development of the community. Other notable buildings include the billiards saloon, the stone schoolhouse, and St. Patrick's Catholic Church.

Vulcan Hotel

The hotel, with only three rooms, is intimate by design and made more so by the personal attention paid by hosts Wendy and Bruce Blakie. They socialize with house guests and local folks in the lounge bar, where knotty-pine tables and an old piano add to the congenial atmosphere. In addition to its darts and pool competitions, the bar also frequently hosts euchre evenings.

St. Bathans is especially popular on New Year's Eve, when locals and visitors carry on the Scottish tradition of "first footing" — going from house to house for a drink. It's not unusual for hundreds of people to attend mass at the Catholic church that night and then ring in the new year at the hotel.

Out-of-towners are drawn not only by the historic hostelry but also by the scenic lake across the road. Blue Lake, as it is called even though recently mineral deposits have turned it green, fills a crater that resulted when gold was recovered from Kildare Hill by a process known as hydraulic elevating. The hill stood nearly four hundred feet high 1864, but after a decade of mining, it had been flattened. By 1936, the abandoned workings had filled with mineral water and become known as the "glory hole."

The hotel has a boat that can be used for waterskiing, and the lake is ideal for swimming.

Wendy and Bruce provide a hearty Kiwi breakfast of fruit, cereal, eggs any style, bacon, sausages, and baked beans. Three-course dinners are available for an extra $8. In the summer months the hosts do barbecue lunches of steak and salads for about $5.

The large oak table, willow-patterned dishes, and lace curtains in the dining room are reminiscent of the period in which the hotel was built.

A vote taken in 1967 also reflected the spirit of the early settlers: a national referendum was held in order to determine whether pub hours should be extended past the traditional six-o'clock closing, and the citizens of St. Bathans voted unanimously in favor of a longer drinking period.

No doubt the miners who formed the town and at one time supported thirteen hotels would have been proud.

Dunedin
and Vicinity

The Scotsmen who settled Dunedin 140 years ago would feel very much at home in their city today. The major public buildings are constructed of large blocks of bluestone, which give the community a handsome appearance and a sturdy, conservative air, and gloomy skies frequently brood overhead.

Larnach Castle, on the Otago Peninsula, was designed in Scotland; Otago University was patterned after Glasgow University. Anglicans may predominate in other Kiwi towns, but the Scots were Presbyterians, and so are their descendants. A kilt maker and a whisky manufacturer add to the Celtic atmosphere.

Dunedin (pop. 107,400) was originally called the New Edinburgh Settlement, and a statue of the Scottish poet Robert Burns can be found in the center of town.

The Scots laid a conservative foundation, but because of Otago University, Dunedin is anything but dull. The students support some of the country's liveliest collegiate pubs and sustain an active program of cultural events.

Invercargill, to the southwest, was also settled by the Scots but lacks Dunedin's appeal and is mainly a commercial center for the surrounding farmlands.

New Zealand's third largest land mass, Stewart Island, has a population of less than five hundred and is an ideal spot for those who enjoy wilderness hiking and camping.

Oamaru, north of Dunedin, is known for its buildings constructed of locally quarried white limestone.

SAHARA GUEST HOUSE

619 George Street
Dunedin, (024) 776-662

■

HOSTS: Paul Brooks and Derek Jay.
LOCATION: Central Dunedin.
CATEGORY: Bed and breakfast inn.
ACCOMMODATIONS: Thirteen rooms, one with
private bath.
RATES: Inexpensive.
INCLUDED: Breakfast.
CREDIT CARDS: All major.

I have an idea of what it must have been like to try to carry on a conversation with Laurel and Hardy because I've talked with their Kiwi counterparts, Derek "Dodger" Jay and Paul Brooks.

Question: "Why is your B & B called the Sahara?"

Answer: "A lot of camels stay here in the quiet season."

Question: "Where did you learn the art of innkeeping?"

Answer: "We watched 'Fawlty Towers' [a BBC comedy rife with hotel faux pas] on telly."

Question: "Why do you keep stuffed rabbits in the glass display case in the dining room?"

Answer: "To keep them from jumping out and eating your muesli."

As hard as I tried, I couldn't get these two comedians to give me a straight answer. Paul has a wild Cockney accent and a great sense of humor; Dodger is his talented straight man.

The hosts are enormously popular with their guests. Paul goes into the parlor at night and chats with everyone, and he makes the rounds again at breakfast. Many visitors enjoy their stay so much they purchase "I've been to the Sahara" sweat shirts and T-shirts emblazoned with the inn's camel, pyramid, and palm tree logo.

The exterior of the B & B is painted bright gold, red, green, and white. The color scheme was inspired by the book *Painted Ladies of San Francisco*, in which colorful Victorian houses are pictured, and initially shocked the residents of this conservative community.

The two-story Victorian, located five blocks from the center of Dunedin, was built in 1865 and from 1947 to 1966 housed the Dunedin Private Hospital.

The Sahara's rooms aren't fancy, but they are spacious and clean. Each has its own hand basin, and five showers and two baths are shared by guests. The dining room and some of the bedrooms have attractive ornamental plaster ceilings. Palm trees, pyramids, and camels are etched into the large frosted window on the landing of the stairway.

The hosts serve a hearty English breakfast that they claim "holds people from one day to the next." "No one who stays here ever has to eat lunch or dinner," Paul assured me.

In spite of this claim, information on local restaurants is readily available. Right next door, Nero's offers a wide range of dishes including enchiladas, pork fillets, and beef stroganoff. Blades, another BYO on George Street, is one of the best restaurants in town. The cuisine includes seafood, poultry, and meat, all prepared with imagination.

The Terrace Cafe on Moray Place is a cozy spot. The Side Walk Cafe (also on Moray Place) is great for lunch. Their self-serve menu includes homemade soup, quiche, casseroles, and a variety of salads.

Dodger and Paul also provide information on sightseeing. One of the main attractions is Olveston, a restored thirty-five-room Jacobean-style mansion that houses a vast collection of art, ceramics, bronze, and silverware.

The town's stone architecture is also of interest, especially the Railway Station and the buildings of Otago Boys High.

In the Octagon in the city center, the musical fountain performs several times a day. Free tours of Cadbury's Chocolate Factory are conducted Monday through Thursday; advance reservations are advised.

On the Otago Peninsula, Larnach's Castle and the Royal Albatross Colony are the most popular features. Access to the colony is limited to certain months of the year, and many visitors are disappointed when they can't see the birds.

Paul's offered to "dress up in a feather suit with a toilet roll on his nose," but so far no one has taken him up on it.

LARNACH LODGE

Larnach Castle, P.O. Box 1350
Dunedin, (024) 761-302

HOSTS: Margaret and Barry Barker.

LOCATION: Otago Peninsula, eight miles east of Dunedin.

CATEGORY: Bed and breakfast inn.

ACCOMMODATIONS: Eleven rooms, four with private bath.

RATES: Moderate.

INCLUDED: Room only.

CREDIT CARDS: All major.

I was tempted to classify Larnach Lodge as a historic hotel because it's located on the grounds of the magnificent neo-Gothic castle built in 1871. However, I realized this would be misleading because the accommodations are only a few years old.

The castle was built by W. J. M. Larnach, a wealthy Australian-born banker and politician who had the means to import Italian marble, exotic timbers, Aberdeen stone, and Venetian glass, as well as skilled artisans from Europe. He enjoyed his home for a time, but in his later years Larnach was beset with financial problems, and he eventually shocked the nation by committing suicide in Parliament House in 1898.

After his death, the beautiful baronial hall he'd created was sold and used to house a variety of institutions, including a mental hospital, a cabaret, and a tourist resort. It was never well maintained, and when Margaret and Barry Barker bought it in 1967 the castle was in a derelict state.

The Barkers have labored continuously for twenty years to restore Larnach's home to its original glory. They've also attended auctions all over the country to buy back the original furnishings of the house. Their efforts were acknowledged when they won the Tourist Design Award in 1982.

Today, visitors pay $3 to roam through the castle's many rooms, resplendent with Venetian glass panels, ormulu-framed mirrors, and embroidered prayer stools. The Georgian hanging staircase and the hundred-foot ballroom remain two of the most notable features.

In 1983 the Barkers constructed Larnach Lodge, a two-story

colonial-style farm building on the grounds of the castle. Four rooms on the second level of the lodge have private baths (showers, no tubs), and seven rooms on the ground floor share bathrooms. Each room has its own coffee and tea facilities.

My favorite is room 26, a corner room upstairs with an antique brass bed, an elegant brocade chaise, and a down quilt covered in a tiny floral pattern to match the curtains. It's not surprising that these quarters are frequently requested by honeymooners.

Everyone accommodated in the lodge shares the magnificent view of the rolling green hills reaching a thousand feet down to Dunedin Harbour on one side and the Pacific Ocean on the other.

Only a brick courtyard and a wide expanse of lush lawn separate the lodge from the castle. Peacocks strutting in the colorful gardens lend an appropriate touch of elegance to the scene. The location is ideal for those who seek peace and quiet and superbly beautiful surroundings.

Because of their rural setting and the lack of public transportation to Dunedin, the Barkers provide all meals for their house guests. Dinners served in the castle cost $15, including a pre-dinner sherry. (Those desiring wine may bring their own.) Breakfasts, morning and afternoon teas, and lunches are available in the tearoom.

Larnach Lodge

One of my nicest New Zealand memories is of a delicious Devonshire cream tea with warm scones fresh from the oven consumed in the castle on an inclement Dunedin day.

Margaret Barker rarely gets to sit down for afternoon tea. Instead, she usually can be found working in the garden or showing visitors a new antique she's just acquired.

One day I asked her how many rooms the castle contains.

"I don't know," she replied. "I've been too busy to count them."

McARTHUR'S HOST FARM

Mataura Island
R.D. 1, Wyndham, (021399) 592
■

HOSTS: Betty and Ian McArthur.

LOCATION: Thirty miles northeast of Invercargill.

CATEGORY: Farm stay.

ACCOMMODATIONS: Two rooms, none with private bath.

RATES: Moderate.

INCLUDED: All meals, wine with dinner.

CREDIT CARDS: None.

Good home cooking awaits Ian and Betty McArthur's house guests. The hosts grow all their own vegetables and use them in creative dishes such as zucchini pie and pumpkin soup. Fresh fruit can be served year-round for breakfast because Betty freezes it when it's in season. Homemade bread is standard fare at lunch time.

The McArthurs' black currants get baked into muffins and pies, and their fresh mint becomes sauce for roast leg of lamb. Betty is generous with her recipes and routinely passes out her directions for preparing Kiwi spring lamb.

Ian and Betty started from scratch thirty-five years ago with "five hundred acres of rabbits." They put up fences, planted trees and a garden, and built their house. Today they successfully farm 2,500 sheep and 100 cattle.

Their comfortable single-story family home has two spacious spare bedrooms for company, one with a double bed and the other with twins; the bathroom (with tub, no shower) is shared with hosts.

Guests are welcome to join in on farm activities or try their hand at trout fishing in the nearby Mataura River. Sometimes the McArthurs take visitors to community events such as a cattle sale or a barbecue with country music.

In addition to farming, both hosts are interested in the stock market, and Betty is a talented spinner and weaver. She demonstrates her craft, and if guests would like to meet a local potter, she takes them over to her neighbor, who has her own wheel and kiln. Every guest receives a lock of sheep's wool as a souvenir.

The hostess also makes her own soap, and her colorful garden is especially nice in spring, when the daffodils and rhododendrons are in bloom.

When families with young children come to stay, Betty takes them to play with her two school-age grandsons. If her house guests are golfers, she is happy to join them for a round.

Ian was in the New Zealand air force in World War II and enjoys reminiscing with other veterans.

McArthur's Host Farm is located on Mataura Island, which isn't an island at all but an area bounded by three rivers. The property is situated in open, rolling country and affords panoramic views — as far as Stewart Island on a clear day.

There is no public transportation to the farm, but new arrivals are collected from the Invercargill airport or the Edendale or Gore bus stations. For those with their own cars, the McArthurs recommend the picturesque southern coast road between Invercargill and Dunedin.

Betty and Ian will take folks on day trips throughout their area for a charge of about $20 per person. New Zealand's first significant dairy factory was built in nearby Edendale, and it was from there that the first exports of cheese were shipped to Britain. Today, visitors can tour a cheese factory and observe its processes.

At home the hosts enjoy sharing their Kiwi beer, wine, and sherry with guests before sitting down to a delicious home-grown dinner.

STEWART ISLAND LODGE

P.O. Box 5
Halfmoon Bay, Stewart Island; Halfmoon Bay 25
■

HOSTS: Jane and Sam Nichol.

LOCATION: Foveaux Strait, thirty-five miles south of Invercargill.

CATEGORY: Country lodge.

ACCOMMODATIONS: Four rooms, all with private bath.

RATES: Moderately expensive.

INCLUDED: All meals, cocktails before dinner, and wine with dinner.

CREDIT CARDS: All major.

The Stewart Island Lodge is a fisherman's dream come true. Sam and Jane Nichol have a forty-five-foot game-fishing launch and enjoy nothing more than a day spent in search of blue cod, groper, trumpeter, moki, or flounder.

Perhaps *search* isn't the right word to use when talking about the abundant waters around Stewart Island. As Sam explained it, "If someone doesn't catch cod, it's because flying pigs got in the way."

The Nichols opened their lodge in 1985 after adding a wing with four comfortable bedrooms to their existing house. Each room has a modern bathroom, attractive decor including original oil paintings, and an outstanding view of Halfmoon Bay and the outlying islands in Foveaux Strait.

Two rooms have double beds, two have twins, and all are centrally heated. A generator provides plenty of electricity, and telephone calls can be made until midnight, when the exchange closes. Coffee and tea facilities are provided en suite, and a big open fire warms the cozy sitting room that visitors share.

Guests and hosts gather around a large circular wooden table for relaxed meals featuring local game and seafood. Jane is a talented chef, and my mouth waters just thinking of a recent dinner she prepared.

We started with pickled mussels, sautéed abalone, and rock-lobster cocktail, which were served with drinks before dinner.

When we went to the table, the hostess presented smoked blue cod as a first course and muttonbird as the entrée. This sea bird is considered a delicacy in New Zealand and, according to law, can only be harvested by Maoris.

Dinner is almost always served in the lodge, but lunch is often eaten on board the boat or on a beach. If passengers gather scallops, mussels, clams (pipis), or other shellfish, Sam lights a fire and barbecues them for the noon meal.

The Toa Tai (Maori for "Ocean Warrior"), the Nichols' launch, can also be used for sightseeing or scuba diving. Fishing equipment, scuba tanks, and weight belts are included in the charter tariff of $17 for a half-day or $28 for a full-day excursion. (Prices are per person and based on a minimum of six people.)

Few residents are as qualified as Sam to conduct tours of Stewart Island and give advice on local activities, because he's been coming to the island for more than twenty years. His father built their house, which the family used as a holiday home, in 1951. Sam and Jane made a permanent move from Invercargill when they decided to open the lodge, but their three teen-agers still attend boarding school there.

In addition to fishing and diving, wilderness hiking, hunting, swimming, bird watching, and flightseeing are popular pastimes.

Most of the Nichols' guests come during the summer months; from August to November the hosts offer a 25 percent off-season discount. At all times of the year, new arrivals and their luggage receive a complimentary transfer from the center of "town" to the lodge, which is only a short distance.

I asked Sam about the best time of year for fishing. His reply was "Year-round."

THE MILL HOUSE

Waianakarua, State Highway One
R.D. 10, Oamaru, (0297) 28-515
■

HOSTS: Joan, Jim, and Grant Wilson.

LOCATION: Fifty-three miles north of Dunedin.

CATEGORY: Historic hotel.

ACCOMMODATIONS: Six rooms, all with private bath.

RATES: Inexpensive.

INCLUDED: Room only.

CREDIT CARDS: All major.

The production of flour was essential to the life of the fledgling colony of New Zealand, and, in spite of the fact that all the metal parts and millstones had to be brought by sailing ship from the other side of the world, thirteen flour mills were constructed in the vicinity of Oamaru in the nineteenth century.

One of these mills was built in 1879 on the north bank of the Waianakarua River. For nearly sixty years a water wheel on this site drove two huge flat millstones, which rotated in opposite directions at differing speeds and created flour out of locally grown wheat. In 1939 the water wheel was burned by patriotic citizens who contributed the iron they recovered to the war effort.

Until 1958, the mill produced poultry feed, and for ten years after that the abandoned building was used as a camp site for Boy Scouts.

Today, a hotel occupies the old mill and provides both a glimpse into history and comfortable accommodations for travelers. The grinding stones are displayed in front of the building, and the original scales used to weigh bags of flour stand in the entrance foyer.

Happily, the river-bank setting remains as picturesque as it must have been in the last century. The original bridge over the Waianakarua, built of locally quarried stone in 1874, is still in use. Several acres of gardens have been added; cherry trees and camellias blossom in the spring, and the rose garden is colorful from November to June.

Grant Wilson and his parents welcome visitors to the Mill

House and go out of their way to make folks comfortable. In addition to six modern bedrooms on the second floor, there is also a cozy television parlor for house guests. Each room has its own coffee and tea facilities and en suite bathroom (with shower, no tub). The outdoor swimming pool is popular in the summer months.

Downstairs, the dining room has a colonial decor, in keeping with the period in which the mill was built. The attractive fireplace is faced with Oamaru stone. Because the walls are three feet thick, the room is warm in winter and cool in summer.

The Mill House is popular with local residents, as well as visitors to New Zealand. On Saturday night the locals come to "dine and dance" and be entertained — often by an elderly lady who plays the electric organ.

The Wilsons' lunch and dinner menus rely heavily on blue cod, orange roughy, and other fish they get from nearby waterfront communities. Because of their location, it's not unusual for fish to be caught in the morning and served at noon on the same day.

Breakfast, accompanied by the morning paper, is brought to the rooms of house guests on a tray.

The mill was restored in 1969 by William Menlove and Bernard Esquilant, who now live in a stone cottage, the former residence of the mill manager, adjacent to the Mill House.

Known as "Bill and Ben, the flower pot men" because of their love of plants, they have developed a delightful garden of rhododendrons, roses, and flowering cherries around their cottage. On the same site they've also opened a tearoom and a gallery that specializes in high-quality New Zealand pottery, paintings, and handicrafts.

The Gallery tearoom serves wonderful morning and afternoon teas, as well as delicious light lunches. On a recent visit I enjoyed homemade country pâté with toast fingers, followed by a shrimp salad and their specialty dessert, Black Velvet Sin.

I'm sure such indulgence would have shocked the strait-laced Victorian settlers, but they might take heart if they could see the English-style gardens that bloom in profusion on the grounds of the flour mill they built more than a hundred years ago.

TOTARA LODGE

299 Thames Highway
Oamaru, (0297) 48-332

■

HOSTS: Isabel and George Custer.

LOCATION: Seventy miles north of Dunedin.

CATEGORY: Bed and breakfast.

ACCOMMODATIONS: Eleven rooms, none with private bath.

RATES: Inexpensive.

INCLUDED: Breakfast.

CREDIT CARDS: All major.

It isn't surprising that the Totara Lodge has a ship-shape appearance. George Custer spent much of his life in the U.S. Navy and only moved to New Zealand with his Kiwi wife after he retired.

George and Issy keep their B & B spotlessly clean but still manage to create a homey, lived-in atmosphere. The contemporary furnishings in the parlor are accented by the hosts' personal belongings, which include an old sewing maching table, an antique clock, a canary, an aquarium full of fish, and lots of house plants. An open fire and a good selection of books and magazines further contribute to the relaxed feeling.

Visitors who go into the parlor to watch television or fix themselves a cup of coffee or tea tend to get drawn into conversation and stay much longer than they expected, because George is very gregarious and enjoys introducing guests to each other.

The eleven bright and cheerful bedrooms have their own sinks and share three bathrooms.

George and Issy met when he was stationed in Christchurch at the navy's Operation Deep Freeze Base (the jumping-off point for Antarctica). She's an Oamaru native, so they returned to her home town after he retired.

The hostess's great cooking contributes heavily to the popularity of the inn. A hearty Kiwi breakfast of spaghetti on toast, baked beans on toast, bacon and eggs, or another specialty is included in the tariff. "All-you-can-eat" dinners are available for an extra $6. These feasts include a salad bar, hot and cold meats, vegetables, and a choice of desserts.

The Totara Lodge is located on the main road, three blocks from the center of Oamaru. The Custers don't pick up new arrivals at the coach or train station, but intercity buses will stop at their gate on request. Off-street parking is available for those with cars.

The single-story B & B was built in 1930 as a private home and offices for a local dentist. In 1963 a large red-brick addition was made and the property was converted to a guest house. Issy has added extensive gardens that flower from October to April.

The hosts direct visitors to sights in the area, which include stately buildings made of Oamaru stone and the Botanical Gardens.

The Totara Estate, located five miles south of town, is also of interest. It was from here that the first shipment of frozen meat was sent to Britain in 1882. The safe delivery of this cargo opened a new era in New Zealand; to this day, shipments like these are a mainstay of the country's economy. The original farm buildings have been restored and are maintained by the Historic Places Trust. Clark's Flour Mill, near Maheno, has also been restored and is open to the public.

The Herbert Forest, just north of Palmerston, has some good picnic spots, walking trails, and scenic drives. The Moeraki boulders and the Karitane blowhole are well worth a detour off Highway 1.

After a day out sightseeing, it's great to go "home" to George and Issy's, where the hosts remember not only the guests' names but also how they take their coffee or tea.

George, a good navy man, drinks his java black.

TARAMEA

Hakataramea Valley
Kurow, (02988) 633
■

HOSTS: Elaine and Rob Grigg.

LOCATION: Thirty-six miles northwest of Oamaru.

CATEGORY: Farm stay.

ACCOMMODATIONS: Two rooms, none with private bath.

RATES: Moderately expensive.

INCLUDED: All meals, wine with dinner.

CREDIT CARDS: None.

The appeal of this farm stay is a combination of charming hosts and the plethora of activities they offer. It's an ideal spot for those with enough time to enjoy both of these aspects.

To begin with, guests are welcome to watch or participate in the normal routines on the Griggs' 860-acre farm. The hosts run 2,500 sheep on part of their property and grow trees, wheat, and barley on the rest. Elaine and Rob take newcomers for a drive over their land and give them an introduction to Kiwi-style agriculture.

Elaine also enjoys taking people around to visit nearby country gardens and to shop for special bargains available in their vicinity. Wool garments are sold at discount prices at a factory in Oamaru. The merino sheep's wool comes from two local farms and is sent to Scotland to be spun and woven. The fabric comes back to New Zealand and is made into expensive clothing.

The other stop for bargain-hunting house guests is at the studio of a friend of Elaine's who designs sweaters and has them hand-knitted to her specifications. These "jerseys," as New Zealanders call them, are sold all over the world, but the Griggs' guests can purchase them directly from the designer.

The hostess also takes those who are interested to see a deer farm, to watch someone spinning wool, and to observe local events such as a cattle sale.

Rob, a gliding instructor, likes to take people up in their two-seater sail plane, and he happily instructs guests in motorbike techniques so they can use the farm bikes to explore the area.

Fishing is another big attraction. From September to April the trout are biting in the Hakataramea River, and in March and April they are joined by hungry salmon in the Waitaki River. The hosts can arrange guides for about $12 an hour, or guests can try their luck on their own.

Elaine prepares whatever fish are caught for dinner and presents them with vegetables fresh from her garden. Non-angling visitors are often served Taramea lamb. All meals are accompanied by good New Zealand wines. During the month of March, just-picked nectarines and peaches are incorporated into the dessert.

The Griggs enjoy lingering at the table, conversing with their company, and, after dinner, playing a game of bridge.

The homestead at Taramea was built in 1919 as a farm cottage and has been added to and remodeled extensively. The decor is similar to that of a British country home, except for one of the guest bedrooms, which is done in shades of slate blue and white and has an attractive early-American look. This room has twin beds, and the larger upstairs room has a double and a single. Two bathrooms are shared by guests and hosts.

Rob and Elaine's home is pleasantly isolated, ideal for those who want to get off the beaten path. Visitors who come by public transportation are picked up at the bus station at Kurow, about seven miles away.

The farm is well placed for those who are driving from Christchurch to Queenstown, and it is especially recommended for travelers who have time for more than an overnight stop.

Christchurch and Vicinity

A flat landscape and picturesque parks and gardens make Christchurch a stroller's city. Some visitors may choose to navigate the Avon River in a rowboat, but many more elect to walk along its willow-lined banks. The Botanical Gardens, some of the best in the world, provide a seemingly endless range for roaming.

The city is the largest in the South Island (pop. 290,000) but still retains the conservative English ambiance its founders envisioned. The tall spire of the Anglican cathedral in the Square can be seen from a great distance. Flower gardens surround even the most humble abodes, and, even in the center of town, life moves at a civilized pace.

Christchurch lies on the level Canterbury Plains, which are bounded on the west by the majestic Southern Alps. The development of the Mount Hutt ski area in these mountains transformed Methven, a nearby farming community, into an accommodation center for winter visitors.

Ashburton (pop. 14,000) is the center of the thriving Mid-Canterbury farming area, and Waimate is a smaller but similar hub in South Canterbury.

Rangiora and Culverden, both in North Canterbury, are set in sheep-raising districts.

Hanmer Springs is an attractive resort based on natural thermal springs, which were discovered by early settlers. In its heyday the town blossomed as a fashionable spa; now it's a pleasant retreat with numerous recreational facilities and a beautiful scenic backdrop.

DARESBURY

67 Fendleton Road
Christchurch; (03) 483-669

■

HOSTS: Ann and Alan Izard.
LOCATION: Central Christchurch.
CATEGORY: Home stay.
ACCOMMODATIONS: Two rooms, each with private bath.
RATES: Expensive.
INCLUDED: Breakfast, dinner, and wine with dinner.
CREDIT CARDS: All major.

The Izards' magnificent three-story Tudor mansion was designed by one of New Zealand's best-known architects, Samuel Hurst Seagar (1854–1933). Seagar is credited with setting a high standard for architectural excellence in Canterbury, the results of which can be seen throughout the province.

The house was built for George Humphreys, a successful businessman and respected member of the community, between 1896 and 1900. The end result of the four-year project was a ten-bedroom home set on a twenty-five acre estate, which also contained a large blue-gum plantation. The trees were popular with rooks, and for nearly fifty years the property was known as Daresbury Rookery.

When the house was built, it was on the outskirts of Christchurch; today, it's only ten minutes from the center of town.

Much of the original land was sold off, but the mansion remained in the Humphreys family until it was purchased by Ann and Alan in 1985.

The hosts have tastefully redecorated many rooms in the house, including the drawing room, which has two fireplaces, handsome antiques, large arrangements of dried flowers, and attractive upholstered settees. French doors open onto a lawn tennis court. A padded window seat provides a view of the swimming pool.

Two and a half acres of grounds surround the house, and a stream flows through the property. The banks of the stream are lined with rhododendrons; ducks waddle back and forth nearby.

The home has for short periods been the South Island residence of two governors general and an archbishop of Canterbury. In addition, Daresbury was visited by King George VI when he was the duke of York. (He came to play tennis.)

The house is registered by the New Zealand Historic Places Trust and is very elegant, but it also has the lived-in feel of a family home. No doubt the Izards' five children, in their late teens and early twenties, contribute to this atmosphere.

Guests at Daresbury are "well looked after," which means they are treated like personal friends and get as much of the hosts' attention as they want. Alan, in particular, enjoys sports with visitors.

One house guest who went jogging with Alan through nearby Hagley Park claimed the run was "the most beautiful in the world."

"Alan will drop anything to play tennis with our company," Ann said, "regardless of the time of year."

The Izards have a rowboat and a canoe, if anyone wants to try their hand on local rivers. The Waimairi, which flows through their property, connects to the Avon River.

Daresbury has a huge billiard room, and Alan enjoys a game with guests. He also plays golf.

For her part, the hostess prepares wonderful four-course dinners, which might start with homemade soup and go on to a first course of smoked salmon and a main course of roast lamb. Ann likes to serve fresh fruit compote with grand marnier for dessert.

Cocktails are served before dinner, and good New Zealand wines are poured during the meal. After dessert, everyone retires to the drawing room for coffee and liqueurs.

A less expensive bed-and-breakfast tariff is offered, but very few people choose that option, since most prefer to dine with their gracious hosts.

Upstairs, two spacious bedrooms are set aside for guests; one has an en suite bath, and the other has a bathroom that is private but not attached.

Mr. Seagar must have had a penchant for unusual plumbing fixtures. All of the showers, baths, bidets, and toilets at Daresbury function quite well, but some of their shapes and sizes are a little out of the ordinary.

ELEVEN CLISSOLD STREET

11 Clissold Street
Christchurch, (03) 554-806
■

HOSTS: Roberta and Alan Conway.
LOCATION: Central Christchurch.
CATEGORY: Home stay.
ACCOMMODATIONS: One room without private bath.
RATES: Moderate.
INCLUDED: Breakfast.
CREDIT CARDS: None.
RESTRICTIONS: No smoking.

American travelers longing for a Yankee breakfast may want to stand up and cheer when they see the meal Roberta Conway offers each morning. Depending on personal preferences, the hostess serves either blueberry pancakes with maple syrup or lox and bagels. The repast is accompanied by perked coffee made from the beans her parents send her from New York.

Roberta has lived in New Zealand since 1970, but she hasn't lost her taste for certain U.S. favorites.

The hostess met her husband when he was teaching American history at Brooklyn College. It was his career that brought them to New Zealand. Since Alan is English, their thirteen-year-old son is the only real Kiwi in the household.

Roberta and Alan roamed the world together before he became confined to a wheelchair, and they enjoy sharing travel experiences with visitors.

"The only complaint we've ever had from house guests," Roberta told me, "is that people find they sit around and talk to us instead of going out sightseeing."

I can easily understand how this could happen, for both hosts are interesting conversationalists. Roberta attended Canterbury University in Christchurch and earned a degree in law. Although she isn't practicing now, she enjoys discussing the differences between the Kiwi and Yankee legal systems. She's also a talented gardener, and both hosts are very well read.

Their comfortable family home, which was built in 1916, has one spacious spare bedroom for guests. Like the rest of the house, this room is furnished with a good assortment of reading material.

The single-story white colonial is located in a pleasant residential area about a twenty-minute walk from town. "There's a bus to the city center," Roberta explained, "but it's faster to walk than to wait for it."

The house is fully equipped for wheelchairs. A ramp leads to the entrance, and the bathroom is accessible.

The hosts enjoy playing bridge with guests, and they also like to help plan onward travels. Since they don't serve lunch or dinner, they stay well informed on the local restaurant scene.

Christchurch has a number of good dining spots, including many ethnic places. Mykonos serves excellent Greek food; Kurashiki, although a trifle expensive, does wonderful Japanese dishes; and Chung Wah is good for Chinese. More traditional Continental fare is offered at the Waitangi Room in Noah's Hotel.

Major Bunbury's, on Colombo Street across from the town hall, is an excellent self-serve carvery for people who want a quick meal in casual surroundings. Dux de Lux, in the Arts Centre, specializes in "vegetarian gourmet" and is also highly recommended.

The Conways' home is near the Merivale Mall, an enclosed shopping center, and within a short distance of several good restaurants.

The central location of Eleven Clissold Street makes it an ideal base for seeing the city. House guests just have to discipline themselves to limit the amount of good coffee and conversation they share with their hosts.

ELIZA'S MANOR HOUSE

82 Bealey Avenue
Christchurch, (03) 68-584

■

HOSTS: Roz and John Smith.

LOCATION: Central Christchurch.

CATEGORY: Bed and breakfast inn.

ACCOMMODATIONS: Eleven rooms, seven with private bath.

RATES: Moderate.

INCLUDED: Breakfast.

CREDIT CARDS: All major.

Christchurch, often called "the most English city outside of England," seems the perfect setting for Roz and John Smith's Elizabethan-style inn. The seven-thousand-square-foot house is set back from tree-lined Beasley Avenue, about fifteen minutes outside of the city center.

The interior has an old-world appearance: bay windows extend the front of the two-story B & B, and high ceilings, wood paneling, and antique furnishings are found in every room. Six fireplaces, several with ceramic tile surrounds, are spread around the house, and wonderful Victorian bric-a-brac rests on the mantles. Brass headboards, wallpaper in diminutive floral prints, and arrangements of dried and fresh flowers are used in most of the bedrooms. Leaded windows and aged photos in gilded frames enhance the atmosphere.

Seven rooms have double beds, and four have twins. The four rooms without private facilities share two bathrooms. One bedroom has wheelchair access.

It's not surprising that Roz and John were attracted to the mansion, with its decidedly British character. Both hosts are from England, where John was a milliner until the couple immigrated to New Zealand by way of Australia.

Their mansion was built for a local government official in 1860. (The kauri timber for the handrails on the impressive staircase was carved in England.) It was used for a time as a boarding house for a girls' college and was at one point divided up into ten apartments.

Roz and John named their property "Eliza's" because when they opened for business, the show *My Fair Lady* was on in Christchurch, and the revamping that Eliza Doolittle went through reminded them of the transformation they'd brought about in the manor house.

The inn is popular with overseas tourists, as well as U.S. navy officers from the Deep Freeze base. When the men aren't "on the ice" in Antarctica, they sometimes stay at Eliza's and talk manager Roz Mulligan into fixing them pancakes for breakfast.

Normally, bacon and eggs, cereal, fruit, toast, and tea and coffee are included in the B & B's tariff. Lunch and dinner aren't served.

During the winter months, when there are fewer travelers in town, the hosts offer an off-season discount rate. Every room has a heater and all beds have electric blankets, so no one gets chilly.

Throughout the year, usually on weekends, the Smiths cater wedding receptions, which are held in the mansion's grand dining hall. Out of consideration for their house guests, Roz and John make sure that any music stops at midnight, and everyone is informed when they make the reservation for their accommodations if a party is scheduled for that night.

Most house guests are out having dinner during the evening hours, and the wedding receptions don't disrupt their plans. Roz and John owned a nearby restaurant, Shakespeare's, before they became innkeepers, so they're a good source of information on dining.

The only impact the wedding parties have on the accommodations is that guests who request the honeymoon suite often find it's already reserved.

WINDSOR HOTEL

52 Armagh Street
Christchurch, (03) 61-503
▪

HOSTS: Carol Healey and Don Evans.

LOCATION: Central Christchurch.

CATEGORY: Bed and breakfast inn.

ACCOMMODATIONS: Forty rooms, none with private bath.

RATES: Inexpensive.

INCLUDED: Breakfast.

CREDIT CARDS: American Express, MasterCard, and Visa.

Of all the B & Bs in New Zealand, I'm sure none does a higher volume of business than the Windsor Hotel. "We average fifty people a night, three hundred and sixty-five nights a year," Don Evans told me.

Even with all these guests, the inn never feels crowded, because there are forty bedrooms and twenty-five bathrooms distributed along the various corridors of the large white two-story building.

The Windsor was built in 1904 as a boarding school. During World War II it became a well-known private hotel, and by the time Don and Carol bought it in 1972, it was once again being used as a student hostel.

The hosts introduced the B & B concept in Christchurch after staying at similar places while traveling in Europe. Their idea of providing clean, inexpensive, friendly accommodations has proven very popular.

In some ways the inn's appearance is reminiscent of its original function as a boarding school. Each bedroom is furnished with chenille bedspreads, print wallpaper, and wall-to-wall carpeting, and the lack of pictures, house plants, antiques, and knickknacks gives the bright and cheery rooms the slightly Spartan feel of a college dormitory.

Don's "Breakfast is served" announcement on the PA system every day might also be regarded by some as collegiate. However, no one complains about the generous morning menu.

The host's reference to the meal as "cowboy tucker" is based on his knowledge of the Old West, which has evolved from watching

John Wayne movies. I'm not sure that even the Duke would have been able to eat all the food that house guests at the Windsor are offered. Juice, fruit, and cereal are followed by a choice of bacon, eggs, sausages, baked beans on toast, or spaghetti.

The bedrooms' lack of coziness is compensated by the homey, comfortable atmosphere of the guests' parlor, where everyone gathers to watch television, have a cup of coffee or tea, and talk.

Because of the inn's size, Carol and Don's contact with their guests is usually limited to greeting each person when they check in, equipping them with maps and sightseeing information, and showing them to their quarters. Instead of chatting with their hosts, house guests tend to converse a lot with each other. Many who meet at breakfast or in the parlor (where Don serves tea and biscuits at nine o'clock each evening) team up for touring the next day.

In addition to cleanliness and budget prices, the central location of the Windsor Hotel contributes heavily to its popularity. Cathedral Square, the heart of Christchurch, is three blocks from the inn's front door. The Arts Centre is two blocks away, and Hagley Park is a five-minute walk. Carol and Don don't serve lunch or dinner, but there are many restaurants in the area.

Windsor Hotel

Size isn't the only factor that makes the inn unique. The fact that 40 percent of its guests are Kiwis is also unusual, because the norm is for B & Bs to have more appeal to overseas travelers.

"And we're also the base hotel for the New Zealand Antarctic Expedition," Don explained. "That's why you see so many guys around here with big, bushy beards.

"The boys are a little spooky when they first come back from the ice, but the other guests seem to enjoy meeting them."

And at the Windsor Hotel there's plenty of room for everyone.

WOLSELEY LODGE

107 Papanui Road
Christchurch; (03) 556-202

■

HOSTS: Shirley and Karl Marxen.
LOCATION: Central Christchurch.
CATEGORY: Bed and breakfast inn.
ACCOMMODATIONS: Fourteen rooms, none with private bath.
RATES: Inexpensive.
INCLUDED: Breakfast.
CREDIT CARDS: American Express, MasterCard, and Visa.

"If you are satisfied, please tell others. If not, please tell us," reads the sign on Karl Marxen's reception desk.

I've seen this notice in other hostelries, but I don't think anyone could mean it as sincerely as Karl does. The host really seems interested in going out of his way for house guests.

To begin with, he picks up new arrivals at the airport, train station, or coach station and transports them back to the B & B free of charge. He also has gone to the trouble of putting black-and-white televisions in each bedroom, in addition to the color set available in the parlor. And his is one of the few bed and breakfast inns I know of that offers lunch (weekends only).

Lunch costs $3, and three-course dinners are available every evening for an extra $6. These evening meals, which are served buffet-style, usually consist of steak, roast beef, lamb chops, or chicken. Karl doesn't pretend that they're gourmet fare, but he told me, "We don't get many complaints."

A hearty Kiwi breakfast is included in the tariff, and coffee and tea are always available in the guests' kitchen. There's also a parlor, and an enclosed verandah on the front of the house is pleasant in summer.

Each of the attractive bedrooms has its own sink, and three bathrooms are shared by residents. The rooms have high ceilings and are spacious and very clean. Room 6 is a nice bright single with three windows facing the street.

The two-story colonial-style house was built as a doctor's residence in 1902 and became a guest house in 1946. The Marxens bought it in 1984.

Karl and Shirley don't live on the premises, but Karl is at the B & B from six-thirty in the morning until seven at night, so he can fix breakfast and dinner and welcome each new guest. In his absence the live-in manager, Pearl Neilson, takes over. Shirley's work as a nurse keeps her from spending much time at the inn.

The B & B is set back from Papanui Road about a half-mile from the city center and is surrounded by trees and shrubs. Off-street parking is provided for travelers with rented (hired) cars.

Both Karl and Pearl counsel visitors about sightseeing in Christchurch. One of the main attractions is the Botanical Gardens, which cover an area of seventy-five acres and include six show houses. It's fun to walk through the gardens, and conducted tours can be taken on an electric trolley called the Toast Rack.

The Canterbury Museum is also a must. Good displays highlight the moa-hunting period of Maori history and Christchurch's colonial era. The exhibits in the Antarctic wing are world-famous.

Those who prefer organized walking to spontaneous meandering should pick up the "Riverside Walk" brochure from the Canterbury Information Centre on Worcester Street. The self-guided excursion passes the cathedral, wanders along the Avon River, and ends not far from the town hall.

Back at the Wolseley Lodge, a sign on the door says *"Haere-mai,"* which means "welcome" in Maori. And Karl backs up those words with a friendly smile and a handshake.

HAWTHORNDEN

2 Hawthornden Road
Christchurch; (03) 585-610

■

HOSTS: Judy and Gordon Neill.
LOCATION: Suburban Christchurch.
CATEGORY: Home stay.
ACCOMMODATIONS: Two rooms, each with private bath.
RATES: Moderately expensive.
INCLUDED: Breakfast, dinner, and wine with dinner.
CREDIT CARDS: None.
RESTRICTIONS: No children.

"Many overseas visitors stay with us just before they leave New Zealand, because we're so close to the airport," Judy Neill explained. "And," she went on to say, "most of them are fairly tired and just want to relax for a day or two before they fly out.

"They sit in the garden and finish up their postcards, and they seem to enjoy talking to us."

In many ways the Neills' attractive white two-story colonial home seems to have been designed with weary tourists in mind. Its proximity to Christchurch International is very convenient, and the twenty acres of park land that surround the house provide the perfect setting for unwinding from a busy trip.

Gordon and Judy keep two hundred sheep and fifty deer on their property, as well as extensive gardens and beautiful native and imported trees.

"We have no cat," Judy told me, "because we like to encourage the birds."

The gardens, which are at their best from October to March, are Judy's "joy and delight." An all-weather tennis court is also set into their spacious lawn.

The interior of the house has the stately look of an English country home. A large stone fireplace is the focal point of the handsome drawing room, which is furnished with a combination of antique and traditional pieces. The dining room, large entrance hall, the kitchen, the sun room, and the cozy den are also on the ground floor.

Upstairs, a billiard room was added when the house was

extended in 1976. Hawthornden was originally built in 1856 for a Scottish immigrant, who planted many of the mature English trees found on the property today. The home was destroyed by fire and rebuilt in 1912.

The Neills purchased the estate in 1980 after retiring from ownership of a high-country sheep station. Their gracious hospitality is one of the main reasons many overseas visitors choose to spend their last days in New Zealand at Hawthornden.

Breakfast and dinner are served in the elegant dining room, and before-dinner cocktails may be enjoyed on the terrace on warm summer evenings. Judy plans the menus around seasonal availability and concentrates primarily on traditional New Zealand dishes.

A typical meal might include homemade seafood chowder, roast lamb, salad, and fresh vegetables from the garden. The hostess's favorite desserts are pavlova and fruit mousse.

Good New Zealand reds and whites accompany the meal, and port is served after dinner in the drawing room. It's not surprising that very few visitors opt for the less expensive bed-and-breakfast tariff.

Accommodations at Hawthornden are spacious bedrooms furnished with English antiques. Each has its own private (but not attached) modern bath. One room has twin beds; the other has a queen and a single. In both rooms, French doors open onto quiet verandahs that provide a view across the tranquil parklike setting.

The house is located five miles from the city center and two miles from the airport. The Neills provide complimentary transfers for departing — or arriving — house guests.

The hosts also enjoy playing tennis or golf with visitors and will happily give advice on their other hobbies: skiing, camping, and fishing. Some guests use Hawthornden as a base for day trips, which include fishing in the Arthur's Pass area, skiing at Mount Hutt, or touring on the Banks Peninsula. (The village of Akaroa, founded on the peninsula in 1840, was the only French colony in the country and retains some of its Gallic atmosphere.)

Regardless of how they spend their time, Judy and Gordon's house guests leave New Zealand with smiles on their faces — and possibly even tears in their eyes.

RAWHITI GUEST HOME

34 Grantly Street
New Brighton, Christchurch, (03) 888-516

■

HOSTS: Suzanne and Peter Coster.

LOCATION: Suburban Christchurch.

CATEGORY: Bed and breakfast inn.

ACCOMMODATIONS: Two rooms share one bath.

RATES: Moderate.

INCLUDED: Breakfast.

CREDIT CARDS: Diners Club, MasterCard, and Visa.

New Brighton, New Zealand, has all the charms of the British seaside resort after which it is named, but it doesn't get as crowded as its English Channel counterpart. Even on a hot day, waves break on a beach only dotted with sun worshipers.

The Rawhiti Guest Home, located about four blocks from the coast, is a good spot for those who prefer ocean breezes to city traffic.

Suzanne and Peter Coster remodeled their single-story family home in 1985 and now have two bedrooms, a bathroom, a sun room, and a parlor available for guests. A full breakfast is included in the tariff, and three-course dinners with wine are offered for an additional $10.

Both of the pretty bedrooms have queen beds covered with colorful quilts. The bathroom is shared between guests (the hosts have their own facilities). The spacious sun room has a tile floor, lots of green plants, and an attractive cane dining table and chairs. Television and coffee and tea facilities are provided in an elegantly furnished visitors' parlor.

The Costers collect new arrivals from the airport, train station, or bus station, and a 10 percent discount applies when people have their own car and don't require transportation. (The B & B's rates are also 20 percent lower in winter.)

On Friday or Saturday nights Peter and Suzanne take interested house guests to the New Brighton Workingman's Club, of which he is a member. This provides a good opportunity for overseas visitors to meet local folks and enjoy the band and dancing.

The Costers' bungalow is located on a quiet residential street adjacent to the Rawhiti Domain's eighteen-hole golf course. The New Brighton Mall, also nearby, has lots of interesting stores and is the only area of Christchurch in which the shops are open after noon on Saturday.

In spite of Suzanne's and Peter's respective occupations as part-time nurse and policeman, they find time to cater to their guests' individual needs. They even take their company shopping on request, and the hostess always manages to turn down the beds at night and keep fresh flowers in each room.

Some visitors spend their days in New Brighton enjoying the beautiful beach, riding the hosts' bicycles, and poking around the shops. Others take the bus five miles into the city center for sightseeing.

Matthews and the Mariner are two good BYO restaurants in the seaside suburb. Queen Elizabeth II Park, the site of the 1974 Commonwealth Games, is also nearby and provides courts for squash and a four-hundred-meter track, as well as a large swimming pool.

New Brighton fortunately lacks the many hotels and tourist attractions of Brighton, England, and instead provides a getaway for those in need of an opportunity to walk barefoot in the sand.

Likewise, the Rawhiti Guest Home provides the comfortable surroundings and friendly hosting that make it easy to sit back and relax.

JASPER LODGE

31 Jackson Street
Methven, (053) 28-019

■

HOSTS: Stephanie and Mike Birch-Jones.
LOCATION: Sixty miles west of Christchurch.
CATEGORY: Bed and breakfast inn.
ACCOMMODATIONS: Three rooms, none with private bath.
RATES: Moderate.
INCLUDED: Breakfast.
CREDIT CARDS: All major.

Overseas visitors who want to ski at Mount Hutt couldn't find better accommodations than with Stephanie and Mike (B. J.) Birch-Jones at Jasper Lodge.

The energetic young pair are both ski instructors on the mountain and seem to know just about all there is to know about the sport. B. J. is from eastern Canada, and Stephanie is a Kiwi; the couple met when both were teaching skiing in Europe.

After they married they returned to New Zealand and bought the colonial villa that, after much hard work, is now their B & B.

The house was built in 1908 as the rectory of the local Catholic church. It later became Mrs. O'Reilly's Boarding House, and when B. J. and Stephanie bought it in 1984, it was in a state of total disrepair. The floors were gone, and most of the windows were broken.

"We pieced together stained-glass windows from broken bits we found around the house and put in new floors," Stephanie told me.

"How did you know how to do it all?" I inquired.

"Well, I'm a Kiwi," she replied, referring to the New Zealand talent for do-it-yourself, "and Mike has studied architecture."

B. J. and Stephanie are justifiably proud of Jasper Lodge. The attractive living room has a brick fireplace in one corner, lots of green plants, a few antiques, and some cane furniture. The eclectic decor imparts a cozy, welcoming feel.

The spacious bedrooms feature comforters covered in Laura Ashley – type prints and Stephanie's trademark — homemade wooden tulips. Each room has a fireplace surrounded by old

ceramic tiles, and kauri woodwork and doors are found throughout the house.

In one bathroom an ancient Singer treadle sewing machine is
used as a plant stand, and the bottle collection they found under
the house is displayed on a windowsill.

In winter, when both are working on the mountain, it takes a
bit of coordination to run the B & B as well. A hearty cooked
breakfast of "B. J.'s special porridge" or eggs, sausages, and hash
browns gives skiers plenty of energy for the day.

Tea is served to everyone when they return to the inn in the
afternoon. Dinner is available for an extra charge of $8.

Mount Hutt is the highest ski area in New Zealand and has the
longest season, often starting in May and running through
November (lift tickets cost $15 a day). Stephanie and B. J. offer
reduced tariffs during the early and late parts of the season.

During the summer, the hosts provide instruction and/or
companionship to people who are interested in river rafting (tame
or wild), canoeing, climbing, horse trekking, cycling, or salmon fishing.

Stephanie is an accomplished horsewoman and can arrange an
all-day ride to Ashley Gorge for $35 including lunch.

The hostess also has a law degree from Otago University, but I
have a feeling it will be a long time before she's able to sit still long
enough to use it.

HAUMOANA

R.D. 7
Ashburton, (053) 23-846
■

HOSTS: Noeline and Leicester Moore.

LOCATION: Sixty-three miles southwest of Christchurch.

CATEGORY: Farm stay.

ACCOMMODATIONS: Three rooms, none with private bath.

RATES: Moderate.

INCLUDED: All meals, wine with dinner.

CREDIT CARDS: None.

Noeline Moore is the consummate Kiwi housewife. She's a superb
cook, wonderful hostess, talented craftsperson, successful garden-

er, and loving mother.

Even in New Zealand, where homemaking skills far surpass those found in other countries, Noeline is unusual. Her guests ooh and ah over her cheesecake and take pictures of her lemon meringue pie and kiwi-fruit trifle, but Noeline seems unaffected by the fuss.

She works alongside her husband on their 440-acre farm, but she still has time to sew, knit, and spin. She breeds her flock of twenty sheep for the color of their wool, which she spins into yarn; she sells the garments she makes.

Because Noeline has two spinning wheels, it's convenient for her to teach this craft to her guests, which she happily does. She also takes orders for knitted clothing from visitors and posts the finished products.

In her "spare" time she grows the vegetables her family and house guests eat and makes kiwi-fruit jam, which is served with scones at tea time.

The Moores began doing farm stays in 1982 after hosting an American Field Service exchange student. "We really enjoyed having him with us," Noeline told me, "and missed him after he left."

I had the feeling, after talking with her, that she and Leicester (pronounced "Lester") probably miss each guest who's ever stayed with them. They remember everyone by name and correspond with many.

Noeline's other interests don't preclude the more mundane housekeeping chores. Their three attractive spare bedrooms, which became available when four grown sons departed, are always clean and neat, as is the rest of their comfortable family home. The bathroom is shared by guests and the hostess.

The single-story brick house was built in 1956 and is surrounded by flower gardens, which are at their best from October to April. "I'm a member of the Ashburton Alpine Garden Club," Noeline said, "but really I'm hooked on dianthus."

The farm was named Haumoana, which means "breeze by the water" in Maori, because of its proximity to the coast. Many house guests enjoy walking on the beach, which is about a mile down the road, and others drive into Ashburton to play golf. There's also good fishing in the area, and the Mount Hutt ski field isn't too far away. The most popular pastime, however, is going out on the farm with the Moores. The hosts devote half of their land to

Romney sheep and use the rest for growing peas, wheat, and barley. Guests can either watch the normal activities or pitch in and help.

Somehow, in spite of all their other activities, Leicester and Noeline still seem to have plenty of time for visitors. They routinely collect new arrivals from the bus station in Ashburton and, for a slight extra charge, will even pick people up in Christchurch.

I wonder if that AFS student realizes how lucky he was to be placed with these warm, friendly, down-to-earth folks?

MOUNT MICHAEL STATION

R.D. 8
Waimate, (0519) 25-589
■

HOSTS: Jo and Calvin Floyd.
LOCATION: One hundred thirty miles southwest of Christchurch.
CATEGORY: Farm stay.
ACCOMMODATIONS: Two rooms share one bath.
RATES: Moderate.
INCLUDED: All meals, wine with dinner.
CREDIT CARDS: None.

Even if I hadn't been told ahead of time, I would have guessed that Mount Michael is the home of an artist. The interior of the early-colonial residence was obviously designed by someone who is both talented and creative. In fact, Jo Floyd is regarded as one of New Zealand's top weavers, and her work is exhibited in galleries throughout the country.

The whole house has the energy that I usually associate with an artist's studio. Colorful ethnic carpets are combined with Georgian, Victorian, and Edwardian antiques. Jo's attractive weavings appear as wall hangings, throw rugs, and cushions. I don't think I've ever seen a home in which color, texture, and shape flow together as well as they do at Mount Michael.

A painting of the Floyds' property done by Robert McDowell, one of the country's best watercolorists, hangs near the fireplace.

A brick-floored foyer with a potbelly stove complements the traditional furnishings in the living room. Jo's studio, dominated by the large loom she bought when she and Calvin were on a teaching exchange in England, is part of the house.

Calvin now teaches at Waimate (pop. 3,400), nine miles from Mount Michael Station. The family also includes two children, a daughter away at school and a charming teen-age son still at home. The Floyds are caring, sensitive people and delightful hosts.

When they have house guests, Jo doesn't weave, so she's free to take people out.

"Or, if they prefer," she said, "I just give visitors a map and point them in the right direction."

Mount Michael is comprised of two thousand acres, on which the Floyds run two thousand sheep. Two goats, Isabel and Gordon, are also an important part of the picture.

On a clear day the view from the guest bedrooms stretches down to the coast. The Hunter Hills form a visual boundary on the other side of the house. (One room has a double bed, and the other has twins; the hosts have their own bathroom.)

Dinners at Mount Michael usually consist of four courses. A typical meal includes homemade soup followed by a first course of fish and an entrée of roast beef and Yorkshire pudding. In the summer Jo likes to serve fresh fruit salad for dessert; in the cooler months apple crumble is her favorite sweet.

Jo will demonstrate weaving if it's requested of her, but she also enjoys going walking with guests. A stream flows through their property, and wallabies roam over nearby hills. In Waimate visitors are welcome on the golf course.

"In addition, we have a pig farmer next door who trains race horses, and some people find that interesting," the hostess said.

More than a half acre of native plants and tree ferns, as well as rhododendrons and camellias, surround the white weatherboard homestead. A swimming pool near the garden is inviting in warm weather.

In terms of both the physical environment and the personalities involved, Mount Michael is a real treat.

MOUNT LAWRY STATION

R.D. 2 Whiterock
Rangiora; (0502) 28-744

∎

HOSTS: Rosemary and Brian Page.

LOCATION: Twenty-eight miles north of Christchurch.

CATEGORY: Farm stay.

ACCOMMODATIONS: Two rooms, each with private bath.

RATES: Moderately expensive.

INCLUDED: All meals, wine with dinner.

CREDIT CARDS: None.

"I much prefer fishing to farm work," Brian confided, "so I really enjoy it when we have anglers staying and they want me to show them where to go."

Not too many Kiwi farmers can leave a five-thousand-acre station to go fishing, but Brian can, because one of his sons helps run the property. When the host is occupied with house guests, Mount Lawry's six thousand Corriedale sheep and two hundred Hereford cattle are in good hands.

Because of this assistance, the Pages are available to accompany visitors "almost anywhere in the South Island."

"Brian got a chauffeur's license," Rosemary told me, "so it's legal for us to take people touring. Of course, we have to charge for it."

Even if they won't be going along, the hosts enjoy helping their guests plan their onward journey. As third- and fourth-generation New Zealanders, they know the back roads well. When I last visited them, they showed me how to travel from their house to Methven without using the main highway. It was a beautiful trip, and I was grateful for their advice.

Sometimes Brian and Rosemary take their company into Christchurch for sightseeing. At other times the guests opt to join in the farm activities.

"We've had people get up at four o'clock in the morning and go out with us for a day's mustering," I was told. "They left in the dark and got back in the dark — and loved it."

Rosemary plays golf with guests and prepares delicious farm-style meals. A typical lunch consists of homemade soup followed by a casserole and cheese and crackers (biscuits). Her three-course dinners feature meat (beef or lamb) and vegetables from their property.

In addition to the sheep and cattle, the Pages raise thorough-bred racehorses and show horses. Guests are not permitted to ride these costly animals, but horseback riding is possible nearby.

Swimming is another popular pastime. The attractive Mount Lawry pool is surrounded by two acres of flowering shrubs. A verandah runs along three sides of the house, providing a good view of the foothills of the Southern Alps and the beautiful rolling countryside.

Rosemary spends a lot of time in the garden, where she has more than a hundred rhododendrons. "We always tell folks to ring [phone] early in the morning or at mealtime," she said, "because I can't hear the telephone when I'm outside."

The Pages' house was built in 1909 by a slightly eccentric heiress. This woman's father had kept her isolated for fear that she would marry and leave him. When she finally did just that, she designed the house on Mount Lawry Station and had it con-structed with an exterior door for every room. I guess that way she felt she could leave whenever she wanted.

The six-thousand-square-foot homestead has two spacious guest bedrooms, both with twin beds. The comfortable living room, with a big fireplace, is the focal point of the family home. The tile on the roof was made in Marseilles and was brought to New Zealand as ballast on ships.

The Pages have been doing farm stays for seventeen years. "We really enjoy having house guests," Brian said.

He didn't add "especially if they want to go fishing," but I bet that's what he was thinking.

LOWRY PEAKS STATION

R.D. 1
Culverden, (0515) 8172
∎

HOSTS: Jocyln and David Davison.

LOCATION: Seventy miles north of Christchurch.

CATEGORY: Farm stay.

ACCOMMODATIONS: Two rooms, each with private bath.

RATES: Expensive.

INCLUDED: All meals, wine with dinner.

CREDIT CARDS: None.

RESTRICTIONS: No children.

When Jocyln Davison was ten years old, her father gave her ten shillings and took her to the antique stores of London's Portobello Road, where she bought her first objet d' art.

I'm sure this little English girl wouldn't have believed for a moment that her purchase would one day rest on a shelf in a glass case in a farm homestead in New Zealand—and that she, too, would live in this house.

I also doubt that when Jocyln visited New Zealand more than ten years ago, she expected to meet a man who would share her interest in fine antiques and English gardens. But that's what happened.

The Davisons' house was built by David's grandfather in 1913 and is elegantly furnished with antiques the couple have purchased at estate sales and auctions around the country. Jocyln's extensive collection of miniatures is on display in the drawing room.

The hostess worked at Bonham's (a fine art dealer in London) before she immigrated to New Zealand in 1977, and her background has made it possible for them to recognize the most precious pieces.

In one of the guest bedrooms the host pointed out a dresser that dates from before 1720; they know this from the way the drawers are made.

Rimu wall paneling and woodwork form a handsome backdrop for the antiques, most of which are Georgian. One exception is a Victorian sideboard that came from David's family.

An English rose garden blooms outside the white weather-board Edwardian home. The nearby pergola is covered with clematis, honeysuckle, and white roses, all of which were chosen for their fragrances. The grounds also include a croquet lawn, a tennis court, and a swimming pool, and the hosts make bicycles (push bikes) available to guests.

From the large sun porch, which Jocyln and David have furnished with cane and wicker furniture, there's a good view over lush farmland to the Southern Alps in the distance.

The Davisons share their interest in gardening and antiques, and they each have their own hobbies as well. Jocyln enjoys china painting and has used her talent to apply delicate floral patterns to the ceramic tiles in one of the guest bathrooms. She appreciates the beautiful dried-flower arrangements done by one of her neighbors and often takes house guests over to see them.

The hostess likes to prepare meals that revolve around fresh, seasonal produce. In the summer the Davisons often barbecue. At any time of the year, "pot chocolate" is the specialty of the house for dessert. Drinks are served before dinner in the drawing room, and good Australian reds and New Zealand whites accompany meals.

David's favorite pastimes are pig hunting and flying in his single-engine Rallye. House guests can accompany him on hunting excursions in the foothills of nearby mountains. For $450 a day, two sportsmen can be supplied with dogs, guns, and a four-wheel-drive vehicle.

The Davisons have two lovely school-age children, Hugo and Charlotte, but, because of their antiques and objets d'art, they don't accept children as house guests.

Many of their possessions are irreplaceable, especially the little treasure purchased for ten shillings many years ago on Porto-bello Road.

THE LODGE

P.O. Box 10
Hanmer Springs, (0515) 7021

■

HOSTS: Diane Richardson and Wally Radford.

LOCATION: Eighty miles north of Christchurch.

CATEGORY: Historic hotel.

ACCOMMODATIONS: Forty-nine rooms, thirty-five with private bath.

RATES: Inexpensive.

INCLUDED: Room only.

CREDIT CARDS: All major.

Early explorers discovered natural hot springs in the Hanmer Plains in 1859. By 1883, a small settlement had grown up around them, and the colonial government, having officially recognized the waters for their "health-giving properties," began encouraging entrepreneurs of the day to build accommodations for people in need of treatment. However, due to various delays, the Lodge didn't open until 1897.

After World War I, the hotel was used temporarily as a hospital for returned soldiers, and in the 1930s a Spanish-style building was erected on the site. It burned to the ground in 1958, but a similarly styled Lodge reopened in 1960.

The large white building is located in the center of Hanmer Springs village, only a few minutes' walk from the thermal pools complex. The curative potential of the hot waters still attracts visitors to the area, but many are also drawn by the region's other features. Some come to play the eighteen-hole golf course at the Hanmer Springs Country Club; others hope to catch brown trout in the Waiau, Clarence, or Acheron rivers. There are also excellent forest walks and guided trail rides. Beautiful mountain peaks encircle the town, which is known for its invigorating climate.

The hotel seems to have something for everyone. In the public bar "locals make strangers welcome" and play darts and pool. Since they aren't allowed to wear them inside, the regular patrons line their gum boots up at the door. They like to "educate" visitors, often retelling the story about the ghost who lives in the Lodge.

The house bar adjacent to the dining room is a pleasant spot for a quiet drink before dinner. The cuisine at the hotel, especially the weekend smorgasbord, is very good and attracts many people to the town. The Garden Restaurant, across the road, is also well known for its tasty fare.

The Lodge has a wonderful old-world atmosphere that, in combination with its remote location, makes it popular with New Zealanders. Only a small portion of the hotel's guests are overseas visitors.

The attractive bedrooms have high ceilings, and some also have iron headboards and oversized bathtubs. (It's sad that, to reduce heating costs, the high ceilings are being lowered as rooms are renovated.)

Three price categories of rooms are available. The least expensive have sinks but no private bath. The medium-priced quarters have a bathroom but no television, and the most expensive (which are still very reasonable) have a private bath, television, and telephone. Breakfast is not included in the tariff, but Continental is available for $3 and a cooked meal costs $4.

The relaxed country atmosphere is conducive to lounging on the lawn with a drink, taking a swim in the hotel's large pool, or playing a friendly game of tennis. In the winter, guests mingle in front of the open fire in the house bar or watch sports on television with the locals in the public bar.

Over the years, the Lodge has hosted more than its share of governors general, members of Parliament, and other notables. In its heyday, the socially prominent came by horse and buggy from Christchurch to stay at the hotel and soak in thermal waters.

Today, Hanmer Springs is much easier to reach, but it remains a haven of fresh air, beautiful scenery, and relaxing pursuits.

APPENDIX

New Zealand Bed and Breakfast Reservation Services

All of the properties profiled in this book can be contacted directly. However, the following list of reservation services is provided for those travelers who would prefer to have an agency book their accommodations. Each farm stay and home stay reservation service has its own list of hosts from which you can choose.

Farm Stays and Home Stays

Farmhouse and Country Home Holidays Ltd., P.O. Box 31250, Auckland, 9, New Zealand. Phone (09) 410–8280.

New Zealand Farm Holidays Ltd., Head Office, Private Bag, Parnell, Auckland, New Zealand. Phone (09) 394–780.

New Zealand Home Hospitality Ltd., P.O. Box 309, Nelson, New Zealand. Phone (054) 82–424.

New Zealand Host Homes Ltd., P.O. Box 60, Russell, Bay of Islands, New Zealand. Phone (0885) 37–658.

New Zealand Travel Hosts, 279 Williams Street, Kaiapoi, Canterbury, New Zealand. Phone (03) 276–340.

Rural Holidays, P.O. Box 2155, Christchurch, New Zealand. Phone (03) 61–919.

Rural Tours, P.O. Box 228, Cambridge, New Zealand. Phone (07127) 5091.

Country Lodges

Hideaway Lodges of New Zealand / Hideaway Connection Limousines, c/o Hoskins Smith Travel, P.O. Box 12, High Street, Auckland, New Zealand. Phone (09) 396–896.

Historic Hotels

Rainbow Adventure Holidays: Pubs for Pennies, 23241 Ventura Boulevard, Suite 216, Woodland Hills, CA 91364. Phone (800) 227–5317 (in California) or (800) 722–2288 (nationwide).

CONCLUSION

During the writing of this book, I've kept in touch with New Zealand by mail and phone in an attempt to ensure that the information you receive is up-to-date.

However, it's possible that as you travel down under you'll discover hosts who have changed their phone numbers, their menus, or — worst of all — their attitudes.

It would be helpful to me to know about any such alterations. I'd also like to hear about your pleasant experiences or any properties you think should be considered for future editions.

Please drop me a note c/o Kiwi Distributors Ltd., P.O. Box 1721, La Jolla, CA 92038. (This address can also be used for ordering copies of *The Woman's Travel Guide To New Zealand*.)

I look forward to hearing from you.

ACKNOWLEDGMENTS

I am indebted to Robert Doughty of United Airlines, Ted Beckett of Mount Cook Airlines, and Bill Hastings of PSA for the assistance they provided.

I also want to acknowledge the invaluable help I received from New Zealand Tourist and Publicity and Hertz of New Zealand.

In addition, my friend Deborah Kenney deserves credit for ably aiding with research.

INDEX